Cubs

Triviology

Christopher Walsh

TRIUMPH
BOOKS

This book is available in quantity at special discounts for your group or organization. For further information, contact:

Triumph Books LLC
814 North Franklin Street
Chicago, Illinois 60610
(312) 676-4247
www.triumphbooks.com

Printed in U.S.A.
ISBN: 978-1-62937-238-9
Design by Meghan Grammer
All photos are courtesy of AP Images.

SPECIAL THANKS
To Noah Amstadter, Tom Bast, Jesse Jordan and everyone else at Triumph Books who worked on this project.

For Cubs fans everywhere

"Chicago Cubs fans are the greatest fans in baseball. They've got to be."

—*Herman Franks*

Contents

One

The Basics

There's history with Major League Baseball, and then there's the Chicago Cubs.

The organization is the very essence of the word tradition, is part of the most established league in professional sports and plays its home games in the National League's oldest venue.

The franchise has been around so long that its initial home was destroyed in the Great Chicago Fire—one of the worst United States disasters in the 19th century. That was 30 years before that other baseball team in Chicago was created and they've been competing for city dominance and more since 1901.

Now that's a rivalry...and that's old by any standard in sports.

Originally formed as an amateur team in 1870, less than a decade after the Civil War, it defeated the St. Louis Unions 47-1 in its first game. A few years later the team became one of the original members of the National League and played its first professional game on April 25, 1876.

To put that into perspective, Colorado, which would add an expansion team in the league 116 years later, would become the 38th state in the union that year. General George Armstrong Custer was killed along with 264 of his Union Calvary after engaging the Sioux tribe at Little Big Horn, and no one cared about the price of gasoline yet because the automobile was still 10 years from being invented.

Ulysses S. Grant was President of the United States, Alexander Graham Bell had just patented the telephone and Mark Twain was in the process of publishing *The Adventures of Tom Sawyer.*

It defeated the Louisville Grays 4–0.

The team's roster that first season was as follows:

Pitcher: Al Spalding.

Catcher: Deacon White.

Infielders: Cap Anson, Ross Barnes, Cal McVey, John Peters.

Outfielders: Bob Addy, Fred Andrus, Oscar Bielaski, John Glenn, Paul Hines.

Owner Tom Ricketts talks with Theo Epstein during 2014 spring training in Mesa, Ariz. (Rick Scuteri)

The Basics

1. When the team was first formed what was its initial nickname?
2. Why was the team first called the "Cubs" in 1902?
3. When did Cubs become the official name of the team?
4. According to the Cubs' media guide the team was known by at least 14 other names between 1887–1913, but which two were the most popular?
5. Name five of the other early nicknames.
6. Who was the franchise's first owner?
7. Which tandem, including a former player, took over in 1882?
8. How much did Charles Murphy pay to purchase the franchise in 1905?
9. Who had financed Murphy's purchase and bought the team in 1914?
10. What Federal League team owner, when that league went under in 1916, purchased the Cubs and merged his teams?
11. What family bought the team and maintained control for more than 50 years?
12. When the Ricketts family purchased 95 percent interest in the Cubs, along with approximately 25 percent interest in Comcast SportsNet in 2009, the transaction was valued as being worth how many dollars?
13. From 1903–42, who did the Cubs play in a semi-annual series after the regular season if the two teams weren't in the World Series?
14. Who is the only manager other than Frank Chance to have a 100-win season?
15. Excluding the 1962 season when the Cubs had three managers (Charlie Metro, El Tappe and Lou Klein), who are the only two managers to endure a 100-loss season?
16. Who is the only player in Cubs history to hit for the cycle more than once?
17. What is the only state that's never had anyone play for the Cubs?
18. Who was named the Cubs' President of Baseball Operations in 2011, and what was his previous claim to fame?

19. Through 2015, what's the only organization to have more regular season wins in Major League history?

20. In its mission statement what is the stated goal of the Cubs' organization?

Answers

1.   The White Stockings, which it kept from 1876–1894

2.   With the new American League raiding the National League for players, many NL clubs stocked their spring training rosters with young, unproven talent. With the team having 20 new players make the team out of spring training, which remains a franchise record, the Chicago Daily News used the nickname "Cubs" for the first time in its March 27, 1902 edition.

3.   1907

4.   Orphans (1898–1902) and Colts (1887–1906).

5.   Black Stockings 1888–1889; Ex-Colts 1898; Rainmakers 1898; Cowboys 1899; Rough Riders 1899–1900; Remnants 1901–1902; Recruits 1902; Panamas 1903; Zephyrs 1905; Nationals 1905–1907; Spuds 1906; Trojans 1913

6.   William Hulbert

7.   Albert Spalding and John Walsh

8. $125,000

9.   Cincinnati Times-Star owner Charles Taft

10. Charles Weeghman

11. The Wrigley family. William Wrigley Jr. purchased control of the team, Philip K. Wrigley took over in 1932 and William Wrigley took control in 1977.

12. $845 million

13. The Chicago White Sox

14. Charlie Grimm in 1935

15. Leo Durocher in 1966 and Dale Sveum in 2012.

16. Jimmy Ryan in 1888 and 1891.

17. Alaska

18. Theo Epstein, who had guided the Boston Red Sox to World Series titles in 2004, their first in 86 years, and 2007. In 2002 he became the youngest general manager in baseball history at the age of 28 years, 11 months, and two years later became the youngest general manager to win a World Series.

19. The New York/San Francisco Giants

20. "The Chicago Cubs' goal is to reward generations of Cubs fans' support and loyalty with a World Championship."

Two

National League History

The history of the Chicago Cubs and the National League are so intertwined that one probably could not have existed without the other.

In 1876 the idea of professional baseball was few years old, but the National Association of Professional Base Ball Players was anything but stable and dominated by one team, the Boston Red Stockings.

In part because five of his star players were on the verge of being kicked out, Chicago businessman William Hulbert started rallying support for the creation of a new league, which became the National League. His own team had suspended play for two years after the Great Chicago Fire, but frustration had grown among owners about the instability of some franchises, suspicions about the influences of gamblers and the lack of a central authority.

It took years for him to convince enough of his peers to get on board for what became known as the Senior Circuit because it was around 25 years before the American League, which for a while it considered inferior.

National League History

1. What was the original name of the National League?
2. Name the original eight teams.
3. Outside of the Cubs which one still exists?
4. Which two organizations were kicked out of the league during the first year, and why?
5. What happened to the other four teams that are no longer in existence?
6. Which two teams that are still in the National League joined in 1883?
7. Where was the first National League game played?
8. How many games was each team scheduled to play?
9. Who had the first hit in National League history?
10. Who is credited with scoring the first run?
11. Who had both the first double and triple?
12. Who had the first home run?
13. Who threw the first no-hitter?
14. What major innovation occurred in 1877?
15. Although many upstart leagues would challenge the National League, which was its first significant rival?
16. Which four teams switched allegiances and joined the National League prior to 1892?
17. When the two leagues essentially merged which four franchises joined the National League in 1892?
18. Which one of those four continues to exist today?
19. When was the first modern World Series played and who won?
20. After the National League existed as an eight-team league for more than 50 years, which expansion team joined along with the New York Mets in 1962?

Answers

1. The National League of Professional Baseball
2. The Boston Red Stockings, Chicago White Stockings, Cincinnati Red Legs, Hartford Dark Blues, Louisville Grays, Philadelphia Athletics, Brooklyn Mutuals and St. Louis Browns
3. The Boston Red Stockings are now the Atlanta Braves. The Cubs are the only original team that never moved.
4. After falling behind in the standings the Athletics and Mutuals refused to make western road trips late in the season, opting to instead play local teams to save money. Hulbert expelled them.
5. Three of them folded within two years. The Cincinnati Red Stockings were expelled after the 1880 season.
6. The New York Gothams and Philadelphia Phillies. The Gothams are now known as the San Francisco Giants.
7. Philadelphia's Jefferson Street Grounds, 25th & Jefferson. Boston defeated the hometown team 6–5.
8. 70
9. Jim O'Rourke
10. Tim McGinley
11. Levi Meyerle
12. Chicago's Ross Barnes. Cincinnati's William "Cherokee" Fisher was the pitcher.
13. St. Louis' George Bradley, against Hartford.
14. Al Spalding made the first major league baseball glove
15. The American Association
16. The teams now known as the Cincinnati Reds, Los Angeles Dodgers, Pittsburgh Pirates and the now-defunct Cleveland Spiders.
17. The Baltimore Orioles, Louisville Colonels, St. Louis Perfectos and the Washington Senators.
18. The St. Louis Perfectos, who became the St. Louis Cardinals. The other three were contracted after the 1899 season. The team now called the Baltimore Orioles were the St. Louis Browns, who moved in 1953.
19. 1903, the Boston Americans of the American League faced the Pittsburgh Pirates of the National League in a best-of-nine series. Boston won the last four games to win the series 5–3.
20. The Houston Colt .45s, who were renamed the Astros in 1965.

Three

Famous Firsts

In addition to winning the first championship during the National League's inaugural year, Chicago arguably had its first dynasty as well.

Cap Anson's team also won three straight pennants from 1880–82, and two more in 1885–86. That 1880 team finished with a record of 67–17, for a .798 winning percentage that will almost certainly never be equaled.

With Frank Chance serving as player-manager from 1905 to 1912, the Cubs won four pennants and two World Series titles over a five-year span. The 1906 team won a record 116 games compared to just 36 losses, good for a .763 winning percentage that's considered the best in Major League history (which goes back to 1901).

Although it lost in the World Series, it's still considered one of the best teams in baseball history, and Chicago came back to win the World Series in 1907 and 1908, becoming the first Major League franchise to play three times in the Fall Classic and the first to win it twice.

Mr. Cub looks out over Wrigley Field. (Leg)

Famous Firsts

1. Who was the first manager in franchise history?
2. Who was the first general manger in Cubs history?
3. Who was the franchise's first batting champion?
4. Who was the Cubs' first home run champion?
5. Who threw the first no-hitter?
6. Who threw the first perfect game?
7. Who threw the first perfect game against the Cubs?
8. Which Cubs pitcher nearly matched him that night?
9. Who was the Cubs' first ERA champion?
10. Who was the first player in the Major Leagues to hit at least 20 doubles, 20 triples and 20 home runs in a single season?
11. Who was the first Cubs player to be named league MVP?
12. Who was the first player in the National League to win back-to-back MVP awards?
13. Who was the first pitcher in baseball history to throw a no-hitter in his first game for a club?
14. Who was the first black player signed by the Cubs?
15. Who ended up being the first black player to appear in a regular-season game for the Cubs?
16. Who was the first black coach in Major League Baseball?
17. Who was the first player to appear in 1,000 consecutive games in the National League?
18. Who's the only Cubs draft selection to make his professional debut with the Major League club?
19. Which team was scheduled to be the opponent for the first official night game at Wrigley Field and which team did it end up being?
20. Who was the first player in Major League history to wear a batting helmet with protective ear flaps?

21. Who was the first Cubs manager to coach a wild-card playoff game?

22. Who was the first player in baseball history to hit five grand slams in a single season?

23. Who was the first Cub to win a Gold Glove Award?

24. Who was the first Cub to win a Silver Slugger Award?

25. Although Frank Robinson was the first black man hired to manage a Major League team, who managed the Cubs on May 8, 1973 after Whitey Lockman's ejection?

Answers

1. Albert Spalding (1876–77)
2. Charles Weber (1934–40)
3. Ross Barnes in 1876.
4. Ned Williamson in 1884. He hit 27.
5. Larry Corcoran on August 19, 1880
6. No one. It hadn't been done through 2015. The one who came closest was Milt Pappas on September 2, 1972, when he issued a walk with two outs in the ninth inning. He still finished with a no-hitter.
7. Sandy Koufax on September 9, 1965.
8. Bob Hendley, who only gave up a bloop double in the seventh inning.
9. Jack Taylor with a 1.33 ERA in 1902
10. Frank "Wildfire" Schulte in 1911
11. Catcher Gabby Hartnett in 1935
12. Ernie Banks in 1958–59.
13. Don Cardwell threw a no-hitter against St. Louis in his Cubs debut May 15, 1960.
14. Gene Baker
15. Ernie Banks
16. Buck O'Neil in 1962
17. Billy Williams
18. Burt Hooton, the second-overall selection in the 1971 draft who made his debut on June 17, 1971 vs. Steve Carlton and the St. Louis Cardinals.
19. The Cubs hosted the Phillies on August 8th, 1988, but the game was rained out prior to playing five innings. So the first official night game occurred the next night, August 9th, against the Mets. The Cubs won 6–4.
20. Ron Santo in 1966.
21. Jim Riggleman in 1998.
22. Ernie Banks in 1955.
23. Ernie Banks in 1960.
24. Leon Durham in 1982.
25. Coach Ernie Banks.

Four

The Stadiums

Before the Cubs joined the National League the team was an independent professional club that played home games at Dexter Park race course or Ogden Park.

Its first permanent home was downtown on the corner of Michigan Avenue and Randolph Street, part of what's now known as Millennium Park. The Union Base-Ball Grounds was also known as White-Stocking Park, and like all other baseball stadiums at the time the stands were mostly made out of wood.

After playing most of the 1871 season there, the Great Chicago Fire on October 8 destroyed the stadium and all the club's possessions. It played the rest of its schedule on the road and in borrowed uniforms.

The team didn't play for the subsequent two years while the city recovered, but eventually returned to the site in 1878 and had home games at Lake Park (which was the name of the whole area along with Lake-Shore Park and Lake Front Park) until 1885.

However, the moving around was not why the team became known as the "Orphans" from 1898–1902. They acquired the nickname after looking lost as a team after Cap Anson was released as a player-manager.

The Stadiums

1. Before Wrigley Field the Cubs played home National League games at five other locations around Chicago. Name them (and if you're from Chicago give the locations).
2. At which did the Cubs have a winning record?
3. What's the address for Wrigley Field?
4. Who also claimed it was their home in a famous movie?
5. By what two names was Wrigley Field called before it was called Wrigley Field?
6. True or false, Wrigley Field was primarily built for the Cubs.
7. How much did it cost to build Wrigley Field?
8. What was the initial seating capacity?
9. Who hit the first home run in stadium history?
10. Which team did the Cubs face when they played their first game there?
11. What was in attendance that day (although not paying, obviously)?
12. What future star hit a grand slam there during his high school championship?
13. Who said: "I'd play for half my salary if I could hit in this dump all the time"?
14. What did the Cubs have a contract to add to Wrigley Field in 1942?
15. Why didn't it happen?
16. For what league did Wrigley Field hold tryouts in 1943?
17. Which football legend made his professional debut at Wrigley Field on Thanksgiving Day, 1925?
18. In 1984 who warned the city of Chicago that all future playoff games involving the Cubs would be moved to St. Louis unless outdoor lights were installed at Wrigley Field?
19. How did Major League Baseball reward Chicago when the Board of Alderman repealed anti-noise laws and approved the addition of lights at Wrigley Field in 1988?

20. In what year was Wrigley Field named Wrigley Field?
21. Which stadium is older, Fenway Park or Wrigley Field?
22. Who went nine innings without giving up a hit at Wrigley Field, only to take a loss to an opposing pitcher who completed the no-hitter?
23. Which famous athlete drove in the winning run in that game?
24. Who did Ernie Banks hit his 500th career home run off of on May 12, 1970?
25. Which opposing player had career hit No. 4,191 at Wrigley Field on September 8, 1985, to tie a major league record?
26. What can be seen over the scoreboard after a win?
27. What can be seen over the scoreboard after a loss?
28. What do some of the other flags signify?
29. What do bleacher fans do when they catch a home run ball hit by an opposing player?
30. Who planted the ivy on the outfield walls?

Answers

1. 23rd Street Grounds (1874–77), 23rd and State streets
   Lakefront Park (1878–1884), South of Randolph Street between Michigan Avenue and Illinois Central Railroad tracks
   West Side Park (1885–1891) Congress and Throop streets
   South Side Park II (1891–1893) 35th and Wentworth streets
   West Side Grounds (1893–1915) Polk and Lincoln (now Wolcott) streets
2. All of them.
3. 1060 W. Addison Street
4. The Blues Brothers used it as their fake address.
5. Weeghman Park and Cubs Park
6. False. It was built to be the home for a team in a third major league known as the Federal League, the Chicago Whales (also called the Federals).
7. $250,000
8. 14,000
9. Catcher Art Wilson of the Federals/Whales
10. The Cincinnati Reds on April 20, 1916. The Cubs won 7–6 in 11 innings.
11. A bear cub
12. Lou Gehrig
13. Babe Ruth
14. Lights

15. The United States military needed the materials during World War II
16. The All-American Girls Professional Baseball League
17. Red Grange
18. Baseball Commissioner Peter Ueberroth
19. Wrigley Field hosted the 1990 All-Star Game.
20. 1926
21. Fenway Park is two years older (1912).
22. Jim "Hippo" Vaughn, who lost to Reds pitcher Fred Toney
23. Jim Thorpe
24. Atlanta's Pat Jarvis
25. Pete Rose. It was a single off Reggie Patterson.
26. A white flag with a blue "W"
27. A blue flag with a white "L"
28. Great individual accomplishments or players including "Hack 191" (Hack Wilson), "66 Sammy" (Sammy Sosa), and "20 KW" (Kerry Wood).
29. Throw it back (or at least a fake ball to make it look like they're throwing it back).
30. Bill Veeck in 1937

Five

Nicknames

What's in a nickname? A lot, especially when it comes to naming a sports organization.

Chicago has been home to some epic and unique franchises, and not just in baseball with the Cubs and White Sox. The Bulls had Michael Jordan, the Bears featured Walter Payton and the Blackhawks were one of the original six franchises in the National Hockey League.

You say Cubs anywhere in the United States and there's no doubt about what team is being discussed. While the "Lovable Losers" tag stuck to describe the faithful fans who continue to root for the team despite not having won a World Series since 1908, so has the "Northsiders" nickname as loyalties in the city are often decided by geography with the White Sox playing on the south side.

Nicknames

Who had the following nicknames?

1. Mr. Cub
2. Husk
3. Ryno
4. Pizza
5. Hank White
6. The Hawk
7. Wild Thing
8. Bull
9. The Human Highlight Reel
10. Crime Dawg
11. Sarge
12. The Penguin
13. Three fingered
14. Superman
15. Spider-Man
16. Rainbow
17. Big Daddy
18. Red Beard (or the Red Baron)
19. The Mad Russian
20. Popeye
21. The Peerless Leader
22. Mad Dog
23. Peanuts
24. Cap
25. Egyptian
26. Death to Flying Things
27. Hippo
28. High Pockets
29. Dim Dom
30. Buy a Vowel

Answers

1. Ernie Banks
2. Frank Chance
3. Ryne Sandberg
4. Ron Santo
5. Henry Blanco
6. Andre Dawson
7. Mitch Williams
8. Leon Durham
9. Mark Prior
10. Fred McGriff
11. Gary Matthews
12. Ron Cey
13. Mordecai Brown

14. Jody Davis
15. Mitch Webster
16. Steve Trout
17. Rick Reuschel
18. Rick Sutcliffe
19. Lou Novikoff
20. Don Zimmer
21. Frank Chance
22. Greg Maddux, who was also known as "The Professor."
23. Harry Lee "Peanuts" Lowrey (he was small as a child and then worked on the Our Gang comedies).
24. Cap Anson. His real name was Adrian Constantine Anson
25. John Healy (he was from Cairo, Illinois).
26. Bob Ferguson
27. James Vaughn
28. George Kelly
29. Dominic Dallessandro
30. Joe Kmak

Ryne Sandberg sips champagne as he and Rick Sutcliffe celebrate clinching the 1984 National League East pennant. (Gene J. Puskar)

Six

The Greats

To many fans there's really just one Chicago Cub who clearly stands out among all the rest: Ernie Banks.

Not only was he considered one of the greatest players of all-time, Banks was on the roster from 1953 to 1971, served as a team ambassador long after he retired and was always active in the Chicago community.

His love affair with the franchise didn't end until Banks died of a heart attack on January 23, 2015, shortly before his 84th birthday.

"Ernie came up through the Negro Leagues, making $7 a day," President Barack Obama said in a statement at the time. "He became the first African-American to play for the Chicago Cubs, and the first number the team retired. Along the way, he became known as much for his 512 home runs and back-to-back National League MVPs as for his cheer, his optimism, and his love of the game. As a Hall-of-Famer, Ernie was an incredible ambassador for baseball, and for the city of Chicago. He was beloved by baseball fans everywhere ..."

"Words cannot express how important Ernie Banks will always be to the Chicago Cubs, the city of Chicago and Major League Baseball," Cubs chairman Tom Ricketts said. "He was one of the greatest players of all time. He was a pioneer in the Major Leagues. And more importantly, he was the warmest and most sincere person I've ever known."

Banks may not have been the first Cub inducted into the National Baseball Hall of Fame, but he has the honor of being listed here first:

 # Ernie Banks

1. Where was Ernie Banks born on January 31, 1931?
2. Why did Banks not play baseball for his high school?
3. Who is credited with having discovered Banks?
4. Where did Banks serve in the military after being drafted by the U.S. Army during the Korean War?
5. During that time what famous team did he play with?
6. Against which team did Ernie Banks make his Major League debut on September 17, 1953?
7. Who beat out Banks for the 1954 National League Rookie of the Year award?
8. In how many consecutive games did Banks play at the start of his career?
9. What snapped the streak?
10. How many home runs did Banks hit in 1955 to set a record for shortstops?
11. What was Banks' career high in home runs?
12. What was his career high in RBIs?
13. Before moving to first base in 1961, what position did Banks briefly move to?
14. How many times was Banks named to the National League's All-Star Team?
15. Who did Banks hit career home run No. 400 off of in 1965?
16. Who gave up Banks' final career home run on August 24, 1971?
17. How many home runs did Banks hit during his illustrious career?
18. As an ordained minister, Banks presided at the wedding of which Major League pitcher?
19. What prestigious award did Banks receive in 2013?
20. Where did Banks die on January 23, 2015?

Answers

1. Dallas, Texas

2. Booker T. Washington High School didn't have a baseball team.

3. Family friend Timothy Gilfoyle, a scout for the Kansas City Monarchs, although others claim it was Cool Papa Bell.

4. In Germany. He served as a flag bearer in the 45th Anti-Aircraft Artillery Battalion at Fort Bliss.

5. The Harlem Globetrotters.

6. The Philadelphia Phillies. He batted seventh in the lineup and went 0-for-3 with a run scored.

7. Wally Moon. The St. Louis Cardinals traded Enos Slaughter to the New York Yankees to make room for him on the roster.

8. 424, which was a record until Hideki Matsui began his career in 2003 and played in 518 consecutive games.

9. A trip to the disabled list due to a hand infection.

10. 44

11. 47 in 1958, when he was named the National League's MVP.

12. 143 in 1959, when he again was named league MVP.

13. Left field. He played 23 games and made only one error.

14. 14

15. Curt Simmons of the St. Louis Cardinals at Wrigley Field.

16. Jim McGlothlin of the Cincinnati Reds

17. 512, 277 of which were as a shortstop, which was a Major League record until it was broken by Cal Ripken Jr. (345).

18. Sean Marshall.

19. He received the Presidential Medal of Freedom. It is the highest civilian award of the United States.

20. Chicago.

Mordecai "Three Finger" Brown in 1912, his last season with the Cubs.

Mordecai Brown

1. What's Mordecai Brown's real full name?
2. Where was he born on October 19, 1876?
3. Why was he called "Three Finger?"
4. How did it help him pitch?
5. How old was Brown when he broke into the majors?
6. With which Major League team did he first play?
7. How many 20-win seasons did he have with the Cubs from 1904–12?
8. What was his career high in wins?
9. Although Brown pitched in two World Series, which game is often called the biggest of his career?
10. Who started that game for the Cubs?
11. Who started for the other team?
12. In what country did Brown play some games in late 1909, only to return home with an unknown sickness?
13. Why was Brown told to give up baseball after the 1912 season?
14. Which team did he play for during the subsequent season?
15. Why did Brown initially leave the Major Leagues?
16. With which Major League team did he return and pitch for in 1916?
17. Who did he face one final time on September 4, 1916?
18. What pitcher with six fingers would play for the Cubs years later?
19. What unusual distinction for a pitcher was Brown as a batter?
20. Who are the only two pitchers in the Hall of Fame with a better ERA than Brown's 2.06?

Answers

1. Mordecai Peter Centennial Brown
2. Nyesville, Indiana
3. Brown lost parts of two fingers as a child in separate farm-machinery accidents.
4. Brown turned this handicap into an advantage by learning how to grip a baseball that would cause an unusual amount of spin. With practice he could make his curveball dramatically break and drop before reaching the plate.
5. 26
6. The St. Louis Cardinals.
7. Six
8. 29 in 1908.
9. The regular-season finale of the 1908 season, a 4–2 victory over the Giants to decide the pennant.
10. Jack Pfiester
11. Christy Mathewson. They faced each other 25 times, Brown had a 13–11–1 record in those games.
12. Cuba
13. A physician told him he risked losing the use of his leg.
14. The Reds. He went 21–11.
15. He jumped to the Federal League and was the player-manager for the St. Louis Terriers in 1914.
16. The Cubs. In 12 games he was 7–2.
17. Christy Mathewson. Mathewson's team, the Reds, won.
18. Antonio Alfonseca
19. He was a switch-hitter.
20. Ed Walsh and Addie Joss

Frank Chance

1. Where was Frank Chance born on September 9, 1876?
2. At what college did he initially enroll?
3. What college did he transfer to and play baseball?
4. Although he probably could have signed with other teams why did he sign with the Cubs?
5. Why did he move to first base?
6. In what statistical category did he lead the National League in 1903?
7. What major change did Chance make in 1905?
8. What did Chance do that led to owner Charles W. Murphy giving him a small stake in the team?
9. In what statistical category is he the Cubs' all-time leader as a player?
10. In what statistical category is he the Cubs' all-time leader as a manager?
11. Who were the two other players Chance formed a famous double-play trio with?
12. In August 1911 why did he suspend one of those players for the rest of the season, only to change his mind two days later?
13. What first was he credited with during Game 3 of the 1910 World Series?
14. When Chance became the game's highest-paid player in 1910, how much did he make?
15. In what sport did Chance compete in during the baseball offseason?
16. In 1912 what risky surgery did he have?
17. What also happened while he was hospitalized?
18. What notable former teammates were inducted into the Hall of Fame along with Chance in 1946?
19. Who played in the first game at Frank Chance Field in Fresno?
20. Name the two other Major League teams he served as a manager.

Answers

1. Salida, California
2. Cal. He planned on becoming a dentist.
3. Washington College in Irvington, California.
4. Tim Donohue was the Cubs' only established catcher on the roster. He saw it as the best opportunity to get playing time.
5. Chance kept suffering finger injuries and in 1903 Johnny King became the Cubs' full-time catcher. Chance still didn't want to switch positions, but received a raise to do so.
6. Stolen bases with 67.
7. When manager Frank Selee became ill he became a player-manager for the Cubs.
8. He stole home from second base in a tie game against the Cincinnati Reds.
9. Stolen bases with 400.
10. Winning percentage.
11. Joe Tinker and Johnny Evers. They were known as "Tinker-to-Evers-to-Chance."
12. He suspended Joe Tinker for using profanity.
13. He was the first player ever ejected from a World Series Game.
14. $25,000
15. Boxing
16. He had surgery to fix blood clots in his brain.
17. He was released by the Cubs, and later signed with the Yankees.
18. Tinker and Evans
19. Joe DiMaggio
20. Red Sox and Yankees in addition to the Los Angeles Angels of the Pacific Coast League. In 1924 he was named the manager of the Chicago White Sox but became ill and never took over. He died later that year at the age of 48.

Kiki Cuyler

1. What was Kiki Cuyler's real name?
2. Where was he born on August 30, 1898?
3. Cuyler's ancestors lived in New York during the 17ᵗʰ century until the start of the Revolutionary War. Where did they move?
4. With which non-Major League team did Cuyler begin his professional career?
5. How old was Cuyler when he played his first game in the Major Leagues?
6. Kiki stems from what name?
7. In August 1925, what did Cuyler do twice in a game at Philadelphia?
8. What makes that accomplishment even more impressive?
9. What was Cuyler's impressive career batting average?
10. In what statistical category did he lead the Major Leagues in 1926, 1928, 1929, and 1930?
11. During that stretch who led the majors in that category the year he didn't, 1927?
12. During which season was he named an All-Star?
13. With which two players did Cuyler form one of the best hitting-outfield combinations of all time?
14. With which team did Cuyler win a World Series?
15. Why did he not play for nearly half of the 1927 season?
16. How was that eventually resolved?
17. What would Cuyler do before stepping into the batter's box to hit?
18. With what team did Cuyler conclude his 18-year career?
19. How old was Cuyler when he died?
20. What business bares his name in his home town?

Answers

1. Hazen Shirley Cuyler
2. Harrisville, Michigan
3. Canada
4. The Bay City Wolves in 1920.
5. 23
6. Kiki is believed to have developed out of his own last name, Cuyler. He was known as "Cuy" and players used to yell that when necessary while making defensive plays, and he also had a stutter.
7. He hit two inside-the-park home runs.
8. The game was played at the Baker Bowl, a very small stadium with a big foul territory (think Fenway Park but smaller).
9. .321
10. Stolen bases
11. Frankie Frisch of the St. Louis Cardinals.
12. 1934
13. Hack Wilson and Riggs Stephenson
14. The Pittsburgh Pirates in 1925.
15. A dispute with manager Donie Bush, who benched him.
16. He was traded to the Cubs for Sparky Adams and Pete Scott.
17. Make the sign of the cross. He was a devout Catholic.
18. The Dodgers.
19. 51
20. Ki Cuyler's Sports Bar & Grill

Johnny Evers

1. In what city was Evers both born on July 21, 1881, and buried after he died?
2. What was his listed height and weight as a player?
3. What did his father do for a living?
4. With which minor-league team did Evers make his professional debut?
5. In what power statistic did he lead the New York State League in 1902?
6. Who discovered Evers?
7. When Evers made his major league debut on September 1, 1902, he was 21 years old. Name the league's only three players who were younger.
8. What two negative things were Evers known for when he was starting out with the Cubs?
9. During the 1904 season he led all National League second basemen in which category: putouts, assists or errors?
10. What important part did he play in the famous play "Merkle's Boner"?
11. In 1908, Evers' .402 on-base percentage was only second in the National League to what player?
12. What caused Evers to miss the end of the 1910 season?
13. What college team did he agree to coach in 1911 over the objections of Cubs manager Frank Chance?
14. What team was he named manager of two years later?
15. Who did the Cubs trade Evers to after firing him as a manager (claiming it still had him under contract)?
16. Which team claimed Evers off waivers in 1917?
17. With which team did Evers agree to serve as player-coach in 1918, but was released before a single game was played?
18. With which team did Evers fill in for injured second baseman Eddie Collins for one game during the 1922 season?

19. With which team did Evers coach, and play an inning for, to be the oldest player in the league in 1929?
20. Why was he called "The Human Crab?"

Answers

1. Troy, New York
2. 5 foot 9, 125 pounds
3. Saloon keeper.
4. The Troy Trojans. At the time he weighed less than 100 pounds.
5. Home runs, with 10.
6. Cubs manager Frank Selee was scouting Evers' teammate, pitcher Alex Hardy, but also needed a second baseman due to an injury to starter Bobby Lowe.
7. Jim St. Vrain, Jimmy Sebring and Lave Winham.
8. His temper and poor defensive play.
9. Actually, he led in all three categories.
10. Evers was the one to alert the umpires to the base-running mistake.
11. Honus Wagner
12. A broken leg
13. The Navy Midshipmen
14. The Chicago Cubs
15. The Boston Braves. In 1914 he won the Chalmers Award, the early version of the National League's MVP award.
16. The Philadelphia Phillies
17. The Boston Red Sox
18. The White Sox. He was 41.
19. The Braves. He was 48.
20. He regularly argued with umpires.

Gabby Hartnett

1. What's Gabby Hartnett's real full name?
2. Where was he born on December 20, 1900?
3. With which team did Hartnett begin his professional career?
4. Which team scouted Hartnett but decided his hands were too small for a Major League catcher?
5. For what catcher was Hartnett signed to serve as backup, only to be traded when he proved to be too valuable?
6. Why did the Cubs call Hartnett "Gabby" during his rookie season?
7. On September 20, 1924 Hartnett caught the 300th career victory for which future Hall of Fame pitcher?
8. How many home runs did he hit in 1925 to set the single-season record for catchers?
9. What statistical category did he also lead National League catchers in that year: errors, putouts, assists or caught stealing percentage?
10. Which team was believed to be trying to trade for Hartnett during the 1925 winter meetings?
11. Between 1928 and 1938, how many times would Hartnett lead National League catchers in fielding percentage?
12. How many times was he named an All-Star?
13. How many times did he catch at least 100 games during a season?
14. How many times did he participate in a double play, setting a National League record for catchers?
15. True or false, Hartnett's 55.74 career caught stealing percentage is the best in Major League history?
16. What moment was considered the pinnacle of Hartnett's career?
17. On August 28, 1939, whose Major League record did he break by playing career game No. 1,727 as a catcher?

18. When he retired, Hartnett's 236 home runs, 1,179 RBIs, 1,912 hits and 396 doubles were all records for catchers. Who broke them?
19. Between Hartnett, Johnny Bench and Yogi Berra who had the best career on-base percentage?
20. For which franchise would he serve as a player-coach in 1941?

Gabby Hartnett has a laugh while relaxing in the dugout during the summer of 1937.

Answers

1. Charles Leo Hartnett
2. Woonsocket, Rhode Island
3. The Nicolet Knights of the Eastern League in 1921.
4. The New York Giants
5. Bob O'Farrell
6. He was shy and didn't talk much.
7. Grover Cleveland Alexander
8. 24
9. He led all of those categories.
10. The New York Giants
11. Seven times
12. Six
13. 12, including a record eight straight.
14. 163. He also set a record for catchers with 452 consecutive chances without committing an error, which has since been broken.
15. False. It's second to Roy Campanella.
16. The homer in the Gloamin', occurred on September 28, 1938 against the Pittsburgh Pirates. Hartnett came to bat with two out in the bottom of the ninth inning and the score tied. With an 0–2 count Hartnett connected on a Mace Brown pitch for a home run that put the Cubs ahead of the Pirates in the standings for first place.
17. Ray Schalk
18. Bill Dickey broke the marks for hits and RBIs in 1943. Yogi Berra topped the home runs mark in 1956, and the doubles record stood until 1983 and Ted Simmons.
19. Hartnett's career on-base percentage was .370, while Yogi Berra's was .348 and Johnny Bench .342.
20. The Giants

Billy Herman

1. What was Billy Herman's full name?
2. Where was he born on July 7, 1909?
3. How old was Herman when he broke in to the majors?
4. True or false, Herman hit a home run during his first plate appearance.
5. In what offensive statistical category did Herman lead the National League in 1935?
6. In what offensive statistical category did Herman lead the National League in 1939?
7. Which number was greater, career walks drawn or strikeouts?
8. Which number was greater, career home runs or career stolen bases?
9. Why did Herman miss two seasons near the end of his career?
10. How many seasons did he hit at least .300 for the Cubs?
11. How many times did he reach the 200-hit milestone?
12. How many times was he named an All-Star?
13. True or false, Herman won a World Series as a player.
14. What two Major League teams did he serve as a manager?
15. With which five organizations was he a coach?
16. For which three teams did Herman play for after the Cubs?
17. What team was Herman talking about when he said, "Why, they've gone and traded the whole team on me?"
18. What National League single-season defensive record does he still hold?
19. Of what Major League single-day record does he have a share?
20. What was Herman's best showing in National League MVP voting, and who won it that year?

Answers
1. William Jennings Bryan Herman
2. New Albany, Indiana
3. 22
4. False as pretty much the opposite occurred. Facing Cincinnati Reds pitcher Si Johnson, Herman knocked the ball into the back of home plate, which then bounced up and hit him in the back of the head, knocking the rookie out.
5. Doubles with 57.
6. Triples with 18.
7. Walks, by a wide margin. He had 737 compared to 428 strikeouts.
8. He hit 47 career home runs and stole 67 bases.
9. World War II.
10. Six
11. Three
12. 10 (1934–43).
13. False, but he did win one as a coach.
14. The Pittsburgh Pirates and Boston Red Sox
15. The Dodgers (1952–57), Braves (1958–59), Red Sox (1960–64), Angels (1967) and Padres (1978–79).
16. The Dodgers, Braves and Pirates.
17. The Pirates after he was acquired and named player-manager in 1946, as part of a deal that sent third baseman Bob Elliott and catcher Hank Camelli to the Boston Braves. Elliott won the 1947 National League's MVP award and led Boston to the 1948 pennant. Herman's 1947 Pirates lost 92 games and he resigned before the season's final game.
18. Most putouts by a second baseman (466).
19. Most hits on Opening Day, with five, set on April 14, 1936.
20. Fourth in 1935, when teammate Gabby Hartnett won the award.

Ferguson Jenkins

1. Where was Ferguson Arthur Jenkins born on December 13, 1942?
2. After taking up baseball as a teenager how would Jenkins hone his pitching skills?
3. With which team did Jenkins make his Major League debut?
4. Jenkins was acquired by the Cubs in 1965 as part of a five-player trade. Name the other four players.
5. During his first full season as a starter with the Cubs, 1967, how many games did Jenkins win?
6. In 1968, when he went 20–15, how many games did Jenkins lose with a 1–0 final score?
7. In 1971, when Jenkins won the Cy Young Award, how many complete games did he throw in 39 appearances?
8. Who did he beat out for the Cy Young Award?
9. How many batters did Jenkins walk that season?
10. How many home runs did he hit in 1971?
11. How many consecutive seasons did Jenkins notch 20 wins with the Cubs?
12. What was Jenkins' career high for wins?
13. Who did he finish second to in 1974 Cy Young voting, but Jenkins beat out for the MVP award?
14. What award did also win that year?
15. Jenkins is one of only four pitchers to ever record 3,000 strikeouts with fewer than 1,000 walks. Name the other three.
16. Who are the only two pitchers to give up more career home runs?
17. Who did Jenkins notch career strikeout No. 3,000 against on May 25, 1982?

Fergie Jenkins pitches during a game at Wrigley Field on April 24, 1983, a day in which he beat the San Francisco Giants to record his 279th career win. (John Swart)

18. Which 1991 game was dedicated in his honor?
19. What league was Jenkins named the commissioner of in 2003?
20. What trophy with his name on it has been missing since then?

Answers

1. Chatham, Ontario.
2. By throwing pieces of coal from a local coal yard, aiming at either an open ice chute or the gaps of passing boxcars.
3. The Philadelphia Phillies
4. Jenkins was traded along with Adolfo Phillips and John Herrnstein to the Cubs for pitchers Larry Jackson and Bob Buhl.
5. 20, while posting a 2.80 ERA and 236 strikeouts.
6. Five
7. 30
8. Tom Seaver
9. Just 37 over 325 innings, compared to 263 strikeouts.
10. Six. He had a .478 slugging percentage and drove in 20 runs in just 115 at-bats.
11. Six (1967–72). It's the longest streak in the Major Leagues since Warren Spahn (1956–61).
12. 25, set with the Texas Rangers in 1974.
13. Catfish Hunter
14. The American League's Comeback Player of the Year.
15. Greg Maddux, Pedro Martinez and Curt Schilling.
16. Robin Roberts and Jamie Moyer.
17. Garry Templeton
18. The 1991 Major League Baseball All-Star Game, held in Toronto. He threw out the ceremonial first pitch.
19. The now-defunct Canadian Baseball League.
20. The Canadian Baseball League's Jenkins Cup.

Michael Kelly

1. Where was Michael Joseph Kelly born on December 31, 1857?
2. Where were both of his parents from?
3. With which team did Kelly begin his Major League career?
4. Despite hitting .348 during his second season, 1879, why was he released from his contract?
5. During his seven years with Chicago how many pennants did it win?
6. What National League offensive category did he lead for three straight years, from 1884 to 1886?
7. What offensive category did he lead the National League in 1884 and 1886?
8. In 1884 Kelly had career-high home runs and RBIs while playing in 108 games. How many did he have of both?
9. What did he do 83 times during his final season with Chicago in 1886?
10. Why did Chicago decide to deal away Kelly?
11. What did it get in return for him?
12. How did Chicago fans react to the news of Kelly being traded?
13. Which organization did he finish his career with in 1893?
14. What was Kelly's career batting average and how many times did he bat better than .300?
15. During his 16-year career how many times did Kelly win a pennant?
16. Which three teams did he serve as a player-manager for?
17. What offensive innovation was Kelly credited with creating?
18. What base-running innovation was Kelly credited with creating?
19. What other well-known activity did Kelly take up after arriving in Boston?
20. Kelly's book *Play Ball* is credited with being the first autobiography by a baseball player. Who ghost wrote it?

Answers

1. Troy, New York
2. They were Irish immigrants.
3. The Cincinnati Reds
4. The Reds ran out of money. Consequently, he essentially became the first high-profile free agent in league history.
5. Five
6. Runs (120, 124 and 155 respectively).
7. Batting average (.354 and .388).
8. 13 home runs and 95 RBIs.
9. Drew a walk, compared to 175 hits and 79 RBIs.
10. He refused to return to the team.
11. $10,000, which at the time was a record.
12. They boycotted the subsequent home opener.
13. The Giants
14. .308 and eight.
15. Eight.
16. The Boston Beaneaters in 1887, he led the Boston Reds to the pennant during the only season of the Players' Leagues in 1890, and led Cincinnati Kelly's Killers (American Association) in 1891.
17. The hit-and-run.
18. The hook slide.
19. Vaudeville performing.
20. *Boston Globe reporter* John Drohan.

Greg Maddux

1. Where was Gregory Alan Maddux born on April 15, 1966?
2. In what country did he spend most of his childhood?
3. Where did he attend high school?
4. Who is credited with having helped Maddux develop his control at a young age?
5. Why didn't Maddux play college baseball?
6. It what round did the Cubs select him in the 1984 draft?
7. In what role did Maddux make his Major League debut?
8. How many wins did Maddux notch during his first full season?
9. How many wins did Maddux notch during his second season, and what Major League record streak did it start?
10. What award did Maddux win 18 times, the most of any pitcher in Major League history?
11. When Maddux couldn't get a deal done with the Cubs and became a free agent in 1992, how big of a contract did he get from the Atlanta Braves?
12. How many World Series titles did Maddux win?
13. Who is the only other pitcher in Major League history to win four straight Cy Young Awards?
14. Who is the only other pitcher Major League history to have more than 300 wins, 3,000 strikeouts and issue fewer than 1,000 walks?
15. How old was Maddux when he re-signed with the Cubs?
16. Where did Maddux notch career win No. 300?
17. Maddux was the first to post back-to-back ERAs under 1.70 in 1994 (1.56 ERA) and 1995 (1.63) since which legendary pitcher?
18. Who is the only pitcher since 1920 to have more career wins?
19. Which team retired Maddux's number first, the Cubs or the Braves?

Answers

1. San Antonio, Texas
2. Spain. Madrid to be specific, where his father was stationed in the Air Force.
3. Valley High School in Las Vegas.
4. Retired major-league scout Ralph Medar.
5. He didn't have many scholarship offers so he declared himself eligible for the draft after graduation.
6. Second
7. He was a pinch-runner in the 17th inning against the Astros on September 3, 1986. He then pitched the 18th and gave up a home run to Billy Hatcher to take the loss.
8. Six, compared to 14 losses, and had a 5.61 ERA.
9. 18, starting a streak of 17 straight seasons in which Maddux won 15 or more games.
10. The Gold Glove Award (1990–2002, 2004–2008).
11. After seven seasons with the Cubs, Maddux signed a five-year, $28 million deal with the Atlanta Braves.
12. One, in 1995.
13. Randy Johnson
14. No one, Maddux is the only one.
15. 38
16. Pacific Bell Park on August 7, 2004, as the Cubs defeated the San Francisco Giants 8–4.
17. Walter Johnson in 1918 (1.27 ERA) and 1919 (1.49).
18. Warren Spahn with 363.
19. The Cubs on May 3, 2009. The Braves did so on July 17, 2009.

Greg Maddux throws a pitch in the first inning of his 300th career win on July 27, 2004. (Morry Gash)

Ryne Sandberg

1. Where was Ryne Sandberg born on September 18, 1959?
2. What did his father do for a living?
3. For whom was he named?
4. In what other sport was he considered a prize prospect?
5. With which school did he sign a letter of intent to play in that other sport?
6. Which team selected him in the 20th round of the 1978 draft?
7. What position did he first play in the Major Leagues?
8. Who was also involved in the trade to bring Sandberg to the Cubs?
9. What position did the Cubs initially want Sandberg to play, where did he play, and then what prompted his move to second base?
10. What major award did he win for the first time in 1983?
11. What major award was Sandberg the first Cubs player to win in 1984 since Ernie Banks in 1958–59?
12. What did he do during "The Sandberg Game" on June 23, 1984? (Bonus: Who hit for the cycle that day but was overshadowed?)
13. What did Sandberg lead the National League in during the 1990 season?
14. How many straight games without an error did Sandberg play to set a Major League record in 1990?
15. What contest did Sandberg also win before the hometown fans in 1990?
16. How many times did Sandberg knock in 100 runs in a season?
17. When he signed a four-year contract extension in 1992, what distinction did Sandberg temporarily achieve?
18. How many Silver Slugger awards did he win?
19. How many times was Sandberg named an All-Star?
20. With which team would Sandberg first serve as a Major League manager?

Answers

1. Spokane, Washington
2. He was a mortician. Sandberg's mom was a nurse.
3. Relief pitcher Ryne Duren.
4. Football. He was named to Parade Magazine's High School All-America football team.
5. Washington State
6. The Philadelphia Phillies
7. Shortstop
8. Sandberg and Larry Bowa were traded to the Cubs for shortstop Iván DeJesús prior to the 1982 season.
9. Center field, third base, and they he switched to second base after the Cubs acquired Ron Cey.
10. The Gold Glove Award. It was the first of nine straight (1983–91)
11. National League MVP
12. Hit home runs in the ninth and 10th innings off St. Louis Cardinals closer Bruce Sutter. Willie McGee hit for the cycle for the Cardinals.
13. Home runs with 40.
14. 123. The record was later broken in 2007 by Plácido Polanco of the Detroit Tigers.
15. The Home Run Derby as part of the 1990 All-Star Game festivities at Wrigley Field.
16. Twice. In both 1990 and 1991 he finished with exactly 100 RBIs.
17. He became the highest paid player in baseball at the time, signing a $28.4 million four-year extension worth $7.1 million a season.
18. Seven
19. 10 (1984–93)
20. The Philadelphia Phillies (2013–15).

Ron Santo

1. Where was Ron Santo born on February 25, 1940?
2. What ailment that he kept quiet about for most of his career was Santo diagnosed with at the age of 18?
3. How did the Cubs acquire him?
4. True or false, Santo was named the National League Rookie of the Year in 1960?
5. What jersey number did Santo initially wear with the Cubs?
6. What defensive team record did he set in 1961?
7. How many times did he lead the league in that category?
8. What single-season Major League record did Santo set in 1965 that still stands?
9. Whose league records for double plays at third base, assistant and total chances did Santo break?
10. Who was the last person to wear No. 10 for the Cubs when it was retired in Santo's honor in 2003?
11. How many Gold Glove Awards did Santo win?
12. What did Santo do 1,071 times during his career, which is still a team record for a right-handed hitter?
13. How many times was Santo named an All-Star?
14. What would Santo do for good luck during the 1969 season?
15. What labor rule was Santo the first to invoke in 1973?
16. Had he not done so, what team would he have ended up with? (Bonus: Name the players the Cubs would have received.)
17. Instead, with which team did Santo play his final season?
18. Which future Cubs icon was part of that deal?
19. How old was Santo when he retired?
20. As a Cubs broadcaster, how did Santo describe himself?

Ron Santo throws out the ceremonial first pitch before the Cubs' 2002 home opener. (Ted S. Warren)

Answers

1. Seattle, Washington
2. Type 1 diabetes.
3. He signed as a free agent in 1959.
4. False. He only hit .251 in 95 games.
5. 15
6. He made 41 double plays at third base, breaking the previous team mark of 33 set by Bernie Friberg in 1923.
7. Six (1961, 1964, 1966–68, 1971), to tie the Major League record held by Heinie Groh.
8. He played in 164 games at third base that season.
9. Eddie Matthews
10. Interim manager Bruce Kimm.
11. Five
12. Draw a walk
13. Nine (1963–1966, 1968, 1969, 1971–1973).
14. A heel click.
15. He was the first player to invoke the ten-and-five rule under the collective bargaining agreement signed after the 1972 Major League Baseball strike. The rule allowed players with ten years service, the last five with the same team, to decline any trade.
16. The California Angels. The Cubs would have received pitchers Andy Hassler and Bruce Heinbechner, who died before the beginning of the 1974 season.
17. The Chicago White Sox
18. Steve Stone, Santo's future broadcast partner with the Cubs.
19. 34
20. As the "single biggest Cubs fan of all time."

Bruce Sutter

1. What's Bruce Sutter's real first name?
2. Where was he born on January 8, 1953?
3. Which team selected Sutter in the 21st round of the June 1970 draft?
4. Instead of signing with that team which college did he briefly attend?
5. In 1977 what was Sutter named to for the first of six times?
6. What did Sutter do on September 8, 1977 while earning a save against Montreal? (Bonus if you can name the three batters he faced in the ninth inning.)
7. How many saves did Sutter record when he won the Cy Young Award in 1979?
8. At the time who was the only other relief pitcher in National League history to win the Cy Young?
9. What ended up being Sutter's career high for saves?
10. Whose Major League record did he tie with that?
11. What caused Sutter to learn how to throw new pitches at the age of 19?
12. After that point what pitch was Sutter especially known for?
13. How many years of eligibility did it take for Sutter to be elected into the Hall of Fame?
14. Sutter was the fourth relief pitcher to be enshrined. Who were the first three?
15. What's the one thing Sutter never did that those three did?
16. How many times did Sutter lead the National League in saves?
17. Who ended up tying his record for consecutive times leading the National League?
18. Sutter retired in 1988 having recorded how many saves?
19. Who are the only two pitchers in Major League history with more?
20. Which team retired his No. 42?

Answers

1. Howard
2. Lancaster, Pennsylvania
3. The Washington Senators
4. Old Dominion
5. The All-Star Game
6. He threw an immaculate inning, throwing exactly nine pitches and all nine were strikes. He retired Ellis Valentine, Gary Carter and Larry Parrish.
7. 37
8. No one had done so, he was the first.
9. 45 in 1984.
10. Dan Quisenberry, who had set the record the previous year.
11. Sutter had surgery on his arm to relieve a pinched nerve
12. The split-finger fastball
13. 13
14. Hoyt Wilhelm (inducted in 1985), Rollie Fingers (1992), and Dennis Eckersley (2004).
15. Start a Major League game.
16. Five (1979, 1980, 1981, 1982, 1984).
17. Craig Kimbrel (2011–14).
18. 300
19. Goose Gossage (302) and Rollie Fingers (341).
20. The St. Louis Cardinals.

Joe Tinker

1. Where was Joe Tinker born on July 27, 1880?
2. True or false, Tinker had a twin sister.
3. Name one of the four minor-league teams Tinker played for before signing with a Major League organization?
4. When Tinker landed offers from two Major League teams, which one did he turn down to sign with the Cubs?
5. In what statistical category did Tinker lead all National League shortstops as a rookie in 1902?
6. In what statistical category did Tinker lead all National League shortstops in 1906?
7. Whom did Tinker stop talking to during the 1905 season?
8. In which of the following offensive categories did Tinker lead the Cubs during the championship 1908 season: hits, home runs, triples, or slugging percentage?
9. In what defensive category did he lead the National League that year?
10. After the season was over, how much of a raise did Tinker ask for?
11. How much more did he get?
12. After the 1910 World Series why did Tinker threaten to quit the Cubs and play baseball in Australia?
13. Which team approached Tinker about becoming its player-manager in 1912?
14. While batting .282 during the 1912 season, Tinker had a career high in which category, runs or RBIs?
15. What move prompted Tinker's departure from the Cubs?
16. To which team was he traded?
17. Why did Tinker miss a significant part of the 1913 season?

18. What did the Brooklyn Dodgers give up to buy Tinker's release from the Reds, with the intent of making him their manager?
19. Why didn't he sign with the Dodgers and instead make the leap to the new Federal League?
20. So how did he end up back with the Cubs in 1916?

Answers

1. Muscotah, Kansas.
2. True, but she died at a young age.
3. The Denver Grizzlies of the Western League (at age 19), the Great Falls Indians and the Helena Senators of the Montana State League, and the Portland Webfoots of the Pacific Northwest League.
4. The Cincinnati Reds
5. Errors with 72.
6. Fielding percentage.
7. Johnny Evers. Although they were part of a famous double-play combination they didn't get along.
8. He led the team in all of those categories with 146 hits, six home runs, 14 triples, and a .391 slugging percentage.
9. He led the league with 570 assists.
10. He was making $1,500 a season and asked for $2,500.
11. $200
12. Salary dispute.
13. The Cincinnati Reds
14. Both, with 80 runs and 75 RBIs.
15. Johnny Evers was named manager. Tinker didn't want to play for him.
16. The Cincinnati Reds
17. He gave blood for his wife's blood transfusion. Despite that Tinker still finished the season with a .317 batting average, .445 slugging percentage, and a .968 fielding percentage, all career highs.
18. $15,000, with another $10,000 to be paid to Tinker (which he never received).
19. Salary dispute.
20. Tinker's team, the Chicago Whales, won the 1915 pennant only to see the Federal League subsequently fold. Charles Weeghman, the owner of the Whales, purchased the Cubs and merged the teams.

Billy Williams

1. Where was Billy Leo Williams born on June 15, 1938?
2. What did his father do for a living?
3. Who predicted that a young Williams would someday win a batting title?
4. Did he?
5. In 1961 who did Williams beat out in National League Rookie of the Year voting?
6. How many home runs did he hit that season?
7. From 1961 to 1973, what was the fewest number of home runs he hit?
8. During that same time span what was his fewest number of RBIs?
9. He had a career number in both categories in 1970. How many home runs and RBIs did he have?
10. In what place did he finish in the National League's MVP voting that year?
11. What epic snub did he get earlier in the 1970 season?
12. What National League record did he set in 1971 that would eventually be broken by Steve Garvey?
13. In what place did Williams finish in the National League's MVP voting in 1972?
14. What accomplishment, which has never been matched in Cubs history, did Williams pull off on July 17, 1966?
15. Where did he do it?
16. What National League single-game record did he tie on April 9, 1969?
17. How many times did Williams hit a home run in a Cubs uniform?
18. Name the team and the opponent when Williams saw his only postseason action as a player.
19. When he fully retired from baseball in 2001, how many seasons had Williams been in a Cubs uniform?
20. What was dedicated in his honor on September 7, 2010?

Billy Williams waves to the fans on "Billy Williams Day," June 29, 1969 in Chicago. (LES)

Answers

1. Whistler, Alabama
2. He was a stevedore.
3. Rogers Hornsby
4. Yes, in 1972.
5. Joe Torre
6. 25
7. 20
8. 84
9. 42 and 129
10. Second
11. The All-Star Game. At the break he was batting .319 with 26 HR and 80 RBIs.
12. Consecutive games played with 1,117.
13. Second again, this time to Johnny Bench. He never did win the award.
14. He hit a natural cycle (single, double, triple and home run in order).
15. Busch Stadium, St. Louis.
16. Four doubles in a game.
17. 392
18. The Oakland A's vs. the Boston Red Sox in the 1975 American League Championship Series.
19. 31
20. A statue of his likeness was dedicated by the Cubs at Wrigley Field, at the corner of Addison Street and Sheffield Avenue.

Hack Wilson

1. What is Hack Wilson's real full name?
2. Where was he born on April 26, 1900?
3. At the age of 16 Wilson left school to do what job that would help his baseball career in a very unusual way?
4. How tall was he and what was his weight for most of his playing career?
5. What setback occurred during his first game as a professional?
6. What position change did this lead to?
7. With which team did Wilson make his Major League debut on September 29, 1923?
8. On July 2, 1925, what Major League record did Wilson tie?
9. Why was Wilson sent to the minor-league Toledo Mud Hens of the American Association later that season?
10. Why would that be a crucial point in his baseball career?
11. What two significant things occurred in Wilson's life on May 24, 1926?
12. In what statistical category did Wilson lead the National League during the 1926 1927 and 1928 seasons?
13. What National League record did he set in 1929?
14. How did he top that in 1930?
15. Why was Wilson awarded another RBI later on?
16. How many home runs did he hit that season?
17. Where did Wilson hit his 200th career home run?
18. When Wilson's career began to decline who did the Cubs trade him to?
19. Who did they turn around and trade him to?
20. Where was Wilson buried after he died broke at the age of 48?

Answers

1. Lewis Robert Wilson
2. Ellwood City, Pennsylvania
3. He swung a sledgehammer at a locomotive factory for $4 dollars a week.
4. 5-foot-6, 195 pounds
5. He broke his leg while sliding into home.
6. He was moved from catcher to outfield.
7. The Giants
8. He hit two home runs in one inning, tying Ken Williams' record set in 1922.
9. He was in a slump, hitting .239 for the season.
10. Due to a front-office mistake he was left unprotected on the Toledo roster and the Cubs claimed him on waivers.
11. He hit the center field scoreboard at Wrigley Field with a home run, and later that night was arrested in a Prohibition-era speakeasy while trying to escape through the rear window. His penalty was a $1 fine.
12. Home runs with 21, 30 and 31, respectively.
13. 159 RBIs.
14. His 190 RBIs set the Major League record.
15. It was discovered that Charlie Grimm had been mistakenly credited with an RBI actually driven home by Wilson during the second game of a doubleheader on July 28. The record of 191 RBIs still stands.
16. 56, which stood as the National League record until 1998.
17. Ebbets Field
18. The St. Louis Cardinals
19. The Brooklyn Dodgers, who released him in 1934.
20. He's buried in the town where he made his professional playing debut, Martinsburg, West Virginia. He had played for the Martinsburg Mountaineers of the Class D (the classification system was different back then) Blue Ridge League.

Seven

Jersey Numbers

Although more than 2,000 players have appeared in at least one game for the Chicago Cubs over their illustrious history, only five numbers have been retired, representing six players who had amazing baseball careers.

The first to be retired was naturally Ernie Banks, the 14-time All-Star who is the Cubs' all-time leader in games played (2,528), at-bats (9,421), and total bases (4,706). Known as "Mr. Cub," his No. 14 will never be worn again.

Following him was Billy Williams' No. 26 in 1987, Ron Santo's No. 10 in 2003, Ryne Sandberg's No. 23 in 2005, and in 2009 the Cubs retired the No. 31 worn by both Ferguson Jenkins and Greg Maddux.

In 1997, Jackie Robinson's No. 42 was retired throughout baseball.

It should be noted that the Cubs didn't start wearing numbers on their uniforms until 1932, having played more than 50 years without them.

Incidentally, according to the Cubs' media guide:

- The most popular last names in Cubs history belong to Smith (16), Johnson (12), Williams (10) and Brown (nine).
- The longest last names in Cubs history, 13 letters each, belong to Gene DeMontreville (1899), Todd Hollandsworth (2004–05) and Ken Raffensberger (1940–41).

- There have been 19 Cubs with last names consisting of three letters, including Derrek Lee (2004–10), Felix Pie (2007- 08), Chad Fox (2005, 2008–09) and Jake Fox (2007, 2009).

 # Jersey Numbers

Give the jersey number for the following players:

1. Larry Bowa
2. Dizzy Dean
3. Kiki Cuyler
4. Hal Jeffcoat
5. Larry Casian
6. Sammy Sosa
7. Shawon Dunston
8. Mark Grace
9. Jeff Samardzija
10. Andre Dawson
11. Joe Garagiola
12. Jerry Morales
13. Roy Smalley
14. Rick Reuschel
15. Rodney Myers

Who were the only people to wear the following numbers for the Cubs?

16. 66
17. 72
18. 74
19. 76
20. 81
21. 94
22. 96
23. 00
24. Who was the first Cubs player to wear No. 99?
25. Who were the first and last people to wear No. 42 on a regular basis for the Cubs?

Answers
1. 1
2. 22
3. 3
4. 19
5. 55
6. 21
7. 12
8. 17
9. 29
10. 8
11. 11
12. 24
13. 39
14. 48
15. 59
16. Rafael Dolis (2011)
17. Robert Machado (2001–02)
18. Thomas Neal (2013)
19. Daniel Garibay (2000)
20. Mike Quade (coach, 2006)
21. Felix Heredia (2001)
22. Bill Voiselle (1950)
23. No one has ever worn it.
24. Todd Hundley in 2001
25. Coach Charley O'Leary was the first in 1932, and Coach Dan Radison was the last (1995–97).

Eight

The Records

When it comes to records that the Chicago Cubs have set over the years, that could be a book by itself.

For example, did you know that the Cubs hold the Major League record for most consecutive seasons without being no-hit? They just missed making it to 50 years when Cole Hamels threw one in his last start for the Phillies (before getting traded to the Texas Rangers) on July 25, 2015.

Or that Mordecai Brown's 48 shutouts during his Cub career (1904–1912, 1916), are 13 more than any other pitcher in franchise history?

How about that Andre Dawson set a Major League record when he was intentionally walked five times by the Cincinnati Reds on May 23, 1990? Although that has to be considered the ultimate compliment, the record-breaking fifth walk loaded the bases in the 16th inning, and Dave Clark followed with a single to give the Cubs a 2–1 victory.

You get the idea. It's difficult figuring out where to draw the line, like with "The Greats" section of this book that includes all of the players who have been inducted into the Hall of Fame and played primarily with the Cubs.

There are numerous other Hall of Fame players and coaches who were with the Cubs at some point but are better associated with other teams. They include:

Induction	Name	Position	Year
1938	Grover Cleveland Alexander	pitcher	1918–26
1942	Rogers Hornsby	second baseman	1929–32
1945	Roger Bresnahan	catcher	1900, 1913–15
1945	Hugh Duffy	outfielder	1888–89
1946	Clark Griffith	executive	1893–1902
1946	Rube Waddell	pitcher	1901
1951	Jimmie Foxx	first baseman	1942, 1944
1953	Dizzy Dean	pitcher	1938–41
1954	Rabbit Maranville	shortstop	1925
1963	John Clarkson	pitcher	1884–87
1964	Burleigh Grimes	pitcher	1932–33
1970	Lou Boudreau	shortstop	1960
1973	Monte Irvin	outfielder	1956
1973	George Kelly	first baseman	1930
1975	Ralph Kiner	outfielder	1953–54
1976	Freddie Lindstrom	third baseman	1935
1976	Robin Roberts	pitcher	1966
1980	Chuck Klein	outfielder	1934–36
1985	Lou Brock	outfielder	1961–64
1985	Hoyt Wilhelm	pitcher	1970
1991	Tony Lazzeri	second baseman	1938
1995	Richie Ashburn	outfielder	1960–61
2004	Dennis Eckersley	pitcher	1984–86
2008	Rich Gossage	pitcher	1988
2010	Andre Dawson	outfielder	1987–92

Moreover, inducted as manager or executive (and played for Cubs or was player-manager) were Tony LaRussa and Albert Spaulding and Hank O'Day, and both Jack Brickhouse and Harry Caray were Ford C. Frick Award recipients as broadcasters.

The Records

1. Who holds the Cubs' career record for games played?
2. Who is the only player in franchise history to have 3,000 hits?
3. Who has the franchise record for home runs?
4. Which two players have struck out the most?
5. Who won the most games as a pitcher?
6. Who has the longest hitting streak in Cubs history?
7. Who has the Cubs record for most hits in a single season?
8. Hack Wilson's 191 RBIs in 1930 is a record that may never be broken, but who are second, third and fourth on the Major League list?
9. What's the team record for scoring in consecutive games?
10. What's the team record for scoring in consecutive games in one season?
11. What's the longest streak in which a Cubs pitcher hasn't notched a shutout?
12. True or false, the Cubs have never played a game in which they scored a run in every inning.
13. True or false, more than one opponent has scored a run in every inning of a game against the Cubs.
14. How many consecutive innings were the Cubs held scoreless during a stretch in the 1968 season to set a National League record?
15. What's the team record for scoring double-digit runs in consecutive games?
16. What National League record did Cubs first baseman Jimmy Collins set on June 29, 1937?
17. Who tied that record on August 15, 2002?
18. What's the Cubs' record for largest last-inning come-from-behind rally?
19. What's the Cubs' record for largest comeback victory?
20. Who owns all National League records for consecutive errorless games at second base?

21. The 2013 team set a franchise record for most players used during a single season. How many players wore a Cubs uniform that season?
22. Through 2015 what's the franchise record for Opening Day runs?
23. What's the Cubs record for Opening Day hits?
24. What's the Cubs highest scoring game in total runs since 1900?
25. Who holds the franchise career record for stealing home plate?

Answers

1. Ernie Banks with 2,528.
2. Cap Anson with 3,081.
3. Sammy Sosa with 545.
4. Sammy Sosa is first with 1,815. Ron Santo is second with 1,271.
5. Charlie Root with 201. He's also pitched in the most games with 605.
6. Bill Dahlen, 42 games in 1894.
7. Rogers Hornsby with 229 in 1929.
8. Lou Gehrig (184), Hank Greenberg (183), and Jimmie Foxx (175).
9. 127, set from June 15, 1958–May 13, 1959.
10. 109, set in 1943 (May 23–September 18).
11. 106 games, set in 1901 (May 18–September 20).
12. False, they did it once during a 36–7 victory at Louisville on June 29, 1897.
13. True
14. 48, June 15–21.
15. Five, set in 1930. The Cubs defeated Pittsburgh 16–4 on June 1 at Wrigley Field, swept the Boston Braves on the road June 3–5 by scores of 15–2, 18–10 and 10–7, and then went to Brooklyn and beat the Dodgers 13–0 on June 6.
16. Zero putouts.
17. Fred McGriff
18. Seven runs, on June 29, 1952, at Cincinnati's Crosley Field. The Cubs went from being down 8–2 to winning 9–8.
19. Nine runs.
20. Darwin Barney
21. 56
22. 16 in both 2005 and 2006.
23. 23, set during a 16–6 victory at Arizona in 2005. Derrek Lee had five RBIs and Aramis Ramirez four.
24. 49, Chicago outlasted Philadelphia 26–23 on August 25, 1922.
25. Frank Schulte with 22.

Andre Dawson watches another home run get out of Wrigley Field in a hurry. (John Swart)

Nine

Quotes

Although Harry Caray had an extensive career in baseball, working 25 years with the St. Louis Cardinals/Browns, 11 with the Chicago White Sox and even one with the Oakland Athletics (1970), his 16 years broadcasting Chicago Cubs games are considered timeless.

He died on February 18, 1998, yet fans and impersonators alike still yell out his trademark lines including: "Hey Everybody," "Holy cow!" and "It could be, it might be, It is! A home run!"

Some of his quips sound like they were made up by comedians ("Did you ever notice that Amaury Telemaco spelled backwards is O'Camelot?"), but the following are honest-to-goodness Caray lines:

"My whole philosophy is to broadcast the way a fan would broadcast."

"I'll tell you what's helped me my entire life. I look at baseball as a game. It's something where people can go out, enjoy and have fun. Nothing more."

"How could (Jorge Orta) lose the ball in the sun, he's from Mexico."

"I know it is the fans that are responsible for me being here. I've always tried in each and every broadcast to serve the fans to the best of my ability."

"It's the fans that need spring training. You gotta get 'em interested. Wake 'em up and let 'em know that their season is coming, the good times are gonna roll."

"I've only been doing this fifty-four years. With a little experience, I might get better."

"I would always sing (Take Me Out To The Ball Game), because I think it's the only song I knew the words to."

"They (Expos fans) discovered 'boo' is pronounced the same in French as it is in English."

"This has been the remarkable thing about the fans in Chicago, they keep drawing an average of a million-three a year, and, when the season's over and they've won their usual seventy-one games, you feel that those fans deserve a medal."

 # Quotes

Name who said the following:

1. "It's a beautiful day for a ballgame ... Let's play two!"
2. "Baseball is a man maker."
3. "All ballplayers want to wind up their careers with the Cubs, Giants or Yankees. They just can't help it."
4. "People always come up and ask me if the Cubs are going to win in their lifetime, and I always give them the same answer: 'How long are you planning on living?'"
5. "We came out of the dugout for Opening Day and saw a fan holding up a sign saying, 'Wait 'Till Next Year.'"
6. "A ballplayer has two reputations, one with the other players and one with the fans. The first is based on ability. The second the newspapers give him."
7. "Look Evers, if you and I talk to each other, we're only going to be fighting all the time so don't talk to me, and I won't talk to you. You play your position, and I'll play mine, and let it go at that."
8. "What, and give him (the batter) a chance to think on my time?"
9. "I never played drunk. Hungover, yes, but never drunk."

10. "I saw him (Al Capone) at the games many times. He was a Cubs fan. Those were rough days in Chicago."

11. "If you don't like Wrigley, you might as well renounce your citizenship right now."

12. "Jack Hamilton could throw a strawberry through a brick wall. If only he could hit the wall."

13. "The longest running daytime soap opera in history, and the only one without a doctor in it."

14. "His strongest playing point was that he was always ready. He could take advantage of a misplay which others wouldn't see until afterward. He played the umpire as intelligently as he did the opposing nine. He would make a friend of him, engage his confidence, and in various ways get the best of close decisions."

15. "If you're going to burn the flag, don't do it in front of me. I've been to too many Veterans' Hospitals and seen too many broken bodies of guys who tried to protect it."

16. "Stan (Hack) really was never given the credit he deserves. He could field bunts as well as anybody and he was a good hitter. I can't understand why he isn't in the Hall of Fame."

17. "Phil (Cavarretta) was the best manager I ever played for. He always spoke his piece, and he knew baseball."

18. "Sam (Jones) had the best curve ball I ever saw. He was quick and fast and that curve was terrific, so big it was like a change of pace. I've seen guys fall down on sweeping curves that became strikes. Righthanders thought Sam had the most wicked curve, and as a left-handed hitter, I thought it was positively the best."

19. "Talent isn't enough. You need common sense and good advice. If anyone tries to tell you different, tell them the story of Hack Wilson. ... Kids in and out of baseball who think because they have talent they have the world by the tail. It isn't so. Kids, don't be too big to accept advice. Don't let what happened to me happen to you."

20. "If (Frank Chance) has to choose between accepting a pair of spikes in a vital part of his anatomy and getting a put-out, or dodging the spikes and losing the put-out, he always takes the put-out."

21. "This team makes your ulcers have a baby."

22. "There's no trying in baseball. You either go out and do it, or you don't."

23. "The groan is audible. It can also be heard."

24. "Greg Maddux could put a baseball through a life saver if you asked him."

25. "People ask me a lot about the values I got from playing for the Cubs for so many years. The value I got out of it was patience. A lot of people these days are not very patient."

26. "There is one thing I will never believe, and that is the Sox are better than the Cubs."

27. "They can't kick you out of the Hall of Fame, can they?"

28. "I'm telling you, nothing destroys a clubhouse more than bad chemistry. Nothing."

29. "I don't care. Just give me the ball. Relievers are trained to react. We're like dogs."

30. "He was electric. He's too young and stupid to understand what he just did. He's just a baby. He's only 20, for crying out loud."

31. "Hank Aaron and Willie Mays and I talk about it all the time. Sammy [Sosa] is the most prolific power hitter we have ever seen. His balance and power and technique and ability to hit the ball to all fields … he is an amazing hitter."

32. "I focus on making that one pitch. That's what I tell myself, "One pitch." You can't worry about the next one. Even with a good hitter, he'll get out seven times out of ten. I want to make sure that this is one of those seven."

33. "I lost the ball in the moon."

34. "When you're eight games behind, it's like eight miles. When you're eight games in front, it's like eight inches."

35. "The only bad thing about being released by the Cubs is that they made me keep my season tickets."

36. "Everything is possible to him who dares."
37. "The first day I walked into Wrigley Field was one of the best days of my life. And I owe them an awful lot."
38. "Ned (Williamson) was the greatest all-around ballplayer the country ever saw."
39. "The challenge is so outstanding, how could you not want to be in this city?"
40. "There's no person alive who got his money's worth better than my old man."

Answers

1. Ernie Banks. He also said while being inducted into the Hall of Fame: "We've got the setting — sunshine, fresh air, the team behind us. So let's play two!"
2. Al Spalding
3. Dizzy Dean
4. Steve Stone
5. Moe Drabowsky
6. Johnny Evers
7. Joe Tinker to Johnny Evers, who supposedly responded "suits me." They never talked again as teammates.
8. Grover Alexander on why he pitched so quickly
9. Hack Wilson
10. Billy Herman
11. Jim Caple
12. Harry Caray
13. Arne Harris
14. Fred Pfeffer on King Kelly
15. Rick Monday
16. Phil Cavarretta
17. Frankie Baumholtz
18. Stan Musial
19. Hack Wilson
20. Christy Mathewson
21. Mark Grace during the 1998 playoff chase.
22. Manny Trillo
23. Harry Caray
24. Joe Morgan
25. Ernie Banks
26. Frank Chance after losing the 1906 World Series to the Chicago White Sox

27. Billy Williams
28. Don Baylor
29. Matt Karchner
30. Mark Grace on Kerry Wood's 20-strikeout game
31. Ernie Banks
32. Tom Gordon
33. Hank Sauer
34. Ron Santo
35. Ken Reitz
36. Al Spalding
37. Bruce Sutter
38. Cap Anson
39. Joe Maddon
40. Skip Caray

Ten

More Than 100 Years, More Than 100 Questions

In 2014, CBSSports.com attempted to piece together an All-Cubs team based solely on single-season performances, which for a franchise with such a rich history wasn't easy:

C: Gabby Hartnett, 1930
1B: Derek Lee, 2005
2B: Rogers Hornsby, 1929
SS: Ernie Banks, 1959
3B: Ron Santo, 1964
LF: Billy Williams, 1972
CF: Hack Wilson, 1930
RF: Sammy Sosa, 2001
SP: Fergie Jenkins, 1971
SP: Pete Alexander, 1920
SP: Mark Prior, 2003
SP: Mordecai Brown, 1906
SP: Greg Maddux, 1992
RP: Bruce Sutter, 1977
RP: Lee Smith, 1983
RP: Carlos Marmol, 2007

That's quite a collection. No Ryne Sandberg, Andre Dawson's 1987 MVP season is not included, nor Rick Sutcliffe's 1984 Cy Young season, and so on.

Regardless, here's a question for every season of Chicago Cubs baseball:

More Than 100 Years

1876 When Chicago went 52–14 to win the pennant during the first year of the National League, name one of the teams to finish second, six games back.

1877 What pitcher finally got a rest after starting 89 consecutive games (most of which were for another team)?

1878 Who led the National League in hits with 100, but didn't have the top batting average?

1879 How many pitchers did the Cubs use during the entire season?

1880 Cap Anson was credited with creating the first pitching rotation using which two players?

1881 On Sept. 27 the smallest paid attendance in Major League history sat through a rainstorm as Chicago defeated the Troy Trojans 10–8. How big was the "crowd?"

1882 How many runs did Chicago score to set a Major League record against the Cleveland Blues?

1883 Which team, now known as the Atlanta Braves, beat out Chicago to win the National League pennant?

1884 Who hit 27 home runs despite having just eight during his first six seasons?

1885 Where did Cap Anson take his team to prepare for the season?

1886   Which pitcher notched his 16th straight win with a 7–3 victory over the New York Giants on July 1?

1887   What pitcher led the National League in games (60), complete games (56), strikeouts (237), and wins (38)?

1888   Who led the National League in hits (182), home runs (16), slugging percentage (.515), and total bases (283), and tied for the most doubles (33)?

1889   Between Frank Dwyer, Ad Gumbert, Bill Hutchison and John Tener, the Cubs had four starting pitchers who posted almost identical numbers, but which one had a losing record at 16–17?

1890   Who at the age of 31 pitched in 71 games, with 66 starts, went 41–25 with a 2.70 ERA?

1891   What did Cap Anson fail to do for the first time during his Major League career, which began in 1876?

1892   Which former Chicago player responded: "Depends on the length of the game," when asked if he ever drank alcohol while playing?

1893   True or false, Chicago played in the first Temple Cup, a new postseason contest that was a best-of-seven series.

1894   Who was credited with helping save 1,600 fans by hacking through a barb-wire fence as a fire spread through the first-base stands during a game against the Cincinnati Reds?

1895   Why was the entire team arrested before a game against the visiting Cleveland Spiders?

1896   Who hit four inside-the-park home runs for the Philadelphia Phillies during a 9–8 victory for Chicago on July 12?

1897   Who led the National League with 73 stolen bases?

1898   Who had a league-leading 1.88 ERA while compiling a 24–10 record?

1899   On October 8th Chicago hosted two different teams for a doubleheader. Name the teams.

1900   Who hit the 20th leadoff home run of his career?

1901   Who struck out 225 batters, but finished with a 10–23 record?

1902   Who had a 1.33 ERA, which was a career best and led the league, while posting a 23–11 record?

1903   Who, when making his debut with the Cubs, formed the first father-son combination in Major League history?

1904   Who set a Major League record by getting hit by a pitch four times during the first game of a doubleheader against the Cincinnati Reds on May 30?

1905   Who stole 59 bases, but only tied for the league lead with Art Devlin of the New York Giants?

1906   How many games did the Cubs win while finishing atop the National League standings?

1907   Why did manager Frank Chance leave Washington Park in New York following a 5–0 victory against the Dodgers in an armored car on July 8?

1908   Who became the first pitcher in Major League history to strike out four batters in one inning in a postseason game?

1909   Who had 32 complete games and won 27 as a starting pitcher for the Cubs?

1910   Who went 20–4 as a starter and led the league with a .844 winning percentage?

1911   Who led the National League in walks (147), on-base percentage (.434), and runs scored?

1912   Who led the league in batting average (.372), doubles (41), hits (207), home runs (14), slugging percentage (.571) and total bases (318)?

1913   On Sept. 14, who set a National League record for most hits allowed (14) while throwing a shutout?

1914   Which pitcher led the team in strikeouts, and the Cubs to the National League lead in the statistical category with 651?

1915   On August 18th, Wilbur Good pulled off an accomplishment that's never been matched in Cubs history. What was it?

1916   Who caught all 27 innings in a doubleheader loss to Pittsburgh on June

28th to set a Major League record?

1917 Why wasn't Hippo Vaughn credited with a no-hitter after he didn't give up a hit through nine innings against the Cincinnati Reds on May 2?

1918 Although Hippo Vaughn led the National League in numerous pitching categories including wins (22), ERA (1.74), shutouts (eight) and strikeouts (148), a teammate had the best winning percentage. Name him.

1919 Who led the National League with a 1.72 ERA and nine shutouts?

1920 Which starting outfielder for the Cubs was listed as being 5 foot 7, and just 149 pounds?

1921 What Giants rookie had a 23-game hitting streak snapped against the Cubs on July 31?

1922 On August 25 the Cubs pulled out a 26–23 victory in a game that featured 51 hits, 23 walks, 10 errors and 25 runners left on base. What team did they beat?

1923 With the Giants visiting the Cubs, what memorable event did Commissioner Judge Kenesaw Mountain Landis witness from the stands?

1924 What first baseman tied a Major League record with 21 putouts during a 9–1 loss against the Brooklyn Dodgers on July 11?

1925 What did the Chicago Cubs start doing on April 14?

1926 Who was the first player to hit a ball off the old scoreboard at Wrigley Field, 475 feet away, on May 23?

1927 Who pulled off an unassisted triple play in the opener of a Memorial Day doubleheader against the Pittsburgh Pirates?

1928 What National League record did the Cubs and Boston Braves combine to set on Sept. 18?

1929 The Cubs' complaint about the ragged sleeve on the pitching arm of a Brooklyn Dodger, which could distract the hitter, led to a rule change that banned the practice. Who was the pitcher?

1930 During Hack Wilson's 191-RBI season which statistical team category between home runs, runs and base on balls did the Cubs not lead the National League?

1931 What happened when player-manager Rogers Hornsby inserted himself into the lineup against the Pittsburgh Pirates on April 24?

1932 Who went 22–6 as a starting pitcher, with a 2.37 ERA and had four shutouts for the Cubs?

1933 What interrupted an exhibition between the Cubs and the New York Giants in Los Angeles on March 11?

1934 Listed as being 6 foot 6, 230 pounds, what position did Jim Weaver play for the Cubs?

1935 What milestone did the Cubs pull off for the last time as a franchise during the 1900s?

1936 Tex Carleton, Larry French, Bill Lee and Lon Warneke all tied for the National League lead for shutouts with three other players. How many did they each have?

1937 Who became the first player in National League history to hit switch home runs (one from both the left and right side) during the same game?

1938 What major batting category (batting average, doubles, triples, home runs, hits, walks, on-base percentage, runs, slugging percentage and stolen bases) did the Cubs lead the National League in while placing first?

1939 Who had a career-high 18 triples to lead the National League, but never had more than 11 during any other season?

1940 Who led the National League with a .317 batting average?

1941 What innovation, something no other Major League ballpark had at the time, was added to Wrigley Field?

1942 On the day shortstop Lennie Merullo committed four errors during a single inning, Sept. 13, against the Boston Braves what other major event occurred in his life?

1943   While Stan Musial dominated most hitting categories, who led the National League with 29 home runs and 128 RBIs?

1944   What would Bill Nicholson be the first player in league history to do, and wouldn't be matched until 1998?

1945   After playing for the Cubs in 1942 and 1944, which baseball legend hit the final two home runs of his career during a doubleheader for the Phillies against the Pirates?

1946   Which pitcher made his first error since 1941, after a record 273 straight chances?

1947   What 5 foot 6 reserve outfielder with a long last name did the Cubs have on the roster?

1948   Why did commissioner Happy Chandler fine the Cubs and two other teams $500 cach?

1949   Who was the only pitcher to have a winning record as the Cubs finished 61–93?

1950   Ron Northey became the first Major League player to do what three times, although only one was with the Cubs?

1951   Who was the first professional athlete to bounce a ball off the center field scoreboard at Wrigley Field? (Note that we did not say that it was a baseball.)

1952   Who struck out 18 Cubs to tie Jim Whitney's single-game record?

1953   Who made his Major League debut and did not miss a game until his consecutive games played streak reached 424?

1954   Among the everyday position players, who was the lone batter who hit from the left side? (Hint: He played first base).

1955   Who just missed notching 200 strikeouts during his first year as a starting pitcher, but still led the National League with 198?

1956   What two atypical Major League records did the Cubs and Giants combine to set during a 17-inning game on May 2, a 6–5 victory for visiting New York?

1957   Why was rookie Dick Drott ejected from a game on April 27?

1958   Which pitcher led the National League in appearances with 69?

1959   What starting pitcher gave up 105 runs, and even more walks, 106, while posting a team-high 16 wins?

1960   Which future manager played second base, third base, shortstop and left field for the Cubs?

1961   How many triples did George Altman hit to lead the National League?

1962   Which team making its debut did the Cubs lose to 11–2?

1963   Who became the first National League player to tally 22 putouts (and 23 chances) in a game, during a May 9th, 3–1 victory over the Pittsburgh Pirates?

1964   Which familiar opponent became only the second team in the modern era to score at least one run in every inning on September 13?

1965   Who had to keep pitching in extra innings to get a no-hitter against the Cubs on August 19, 1965?

1966   Who was traded away by the Cubs only to throw five shutouts for the Philadelphia Phillies?

1967   During the second game of a June 11th doubleheader, the Cubs and what opponent combined to tie a Major League record with 11 home runs? (Bonus: Name the teams that set the mark in 1950.)

1968   Who led the National League in runs scored with 98?

1969   Who hit two three-run home runs and also had a double en route to seven RBIs during a 19–0 victory over the San Diego Padres on May 13?

1970   Which team edged the Cubs to win the National League East Division title?

1971   Who threw the pitch that hit Ron Hunt, putting the Montreal Expo in the Major League record book for being hit by 50 pitches?

1972   Who threw a no-hitter against the Phillies on April 16 during just his fourth game in the major leagues?

Sammy Sosa and Mark Grace pose with Harry Caray at the opening ceremonies of the 1994 Cubs Fan Convention. (John Swart)

1973   With the team about to start looking more toward its future and trade away a lot of its top players, name one of the four regulars who played together for the final time on October 1.

1974   Who had a base salary of $150,000 while none of the other Cubs made more than $32,500? (Bonus: Name the person with the second-biggest salary.)

1975   Who became the first modern player to notch seven hits in a single nine-inning game during a 22–0 victory against the Cubs?

1976   What opponent hit four home runs during an 18–16 victory at Wrigley Field on April 17?

1977   Who was the Cubs' 20-game winner?

1978   How many players did Herman Franks and Montreal Expos manager Dick Williams combine to use in a nine-inning game to set a Major League record?

1979   Who led the National League with 48 home runs and a .613 slugging percentage?

1980   Who led the National League with a .324 batting average?

1981   Who with a soon-to-be famous name for other reasons was a 5 foot 9 reserve second baseman for the Cubs?

1982   Who did Fergie Jenkins strike out to become just the seventh pitcher to fan 3,000 batters?

1983   What pitcher appeared in 82 games for the Cubs?

1984   What did the Cubs do for the first time since 1945?

1985   True or false, while the Cubs didn't finish atop the East Division they did have the biggest payroll in the National League.

1986   Who did the Cubs fire for "behavior unbecoming an employee" of the franchise?

1987   Who became the first player to ever win the Most Valuable Player Award with a last-place team?

1988   Who did the Cubs host August 9 for the first night game played at Wrigley Field?

1989   Which pitcher led the National League in appearances with 76?

1990   What Major League record did Greg Maddux set for pitchers during a 4–0 victory against the Los Angeles Dodgers?

1991   After Andre Dawson hit a grand slam in the 11th inning, what record did the Pittsburgh Pirates set on April 21?

1992   Who tried to move the Cubs, only to be overruled by Major League Baseball's executive council?

1993   What opposing player left the dugout and watched the ongoing game with fans on the roof of a three-story building on Sheffield Avenue overlooking Wrigley Field on July 7?

1994   Who became the first National League player to hit three home runs, all
       consecutive, on Opening Day? (Bonus: Who was the pitcher?)
1995   Which number was greater, the number of doubles Mark Grace hit to
       lead the National League, or the number of saves Randy Myers notched
       to top the league?
1996   Which opposing player became the first South Korean pitcher to win a
       game in the Major Leagues?
1997   Who led the Cubs in wins with 11?
1998   Who gave up Mark McGwire's 62nd home run of the season?
1999   Who was the only starting pitcher to notch double-digit wins?
2000   Where did the Cubs open the season, and which team did they face in
       the first regular-season game ever played outside of North America?
2001   What franchise single-season record did the Cubs set with 1,344?
2002   While Matt Clement and Kerry Wood had almost identical stat lines, both
       going 12–11, which two pitchers had the next most wins with six?
2003   Who was ejected, and later suspended for seven games, after umpires
       found cork in his shattered bat during a game with the Tampa Bay
       Devil Rays?
2004   Who became the first National League pitcher since Steve Carlton in
       1983 to join the 300-win club?
2005   Which franchise did the Cubs tie for the most consecutive seasons
       (97) without winning the World Series?
2006   Who hit four doubles in a single game for the Cubs?
2007   Who went 18–13, with a 3.95 ERA and struck out 177 batters
       while also walking 101?
2008   Although the Cubs and the White Sox first played each other in
       the 1906 World Series, what did they do for the first time 102
       years later?
2009   Which three starting pitchers reached double digits in wins?
2010   Who did the Cubs lose to when playing the 20,000th game in franchise
       history on June 26th?

2011   During just his second season with the Cubs, who had 207 hits to lead the National League?

2012   Even though the Cubs lost 101 games, which team finished below them in the National League Central standings?

2013   How many home losses did the Cubs have to set a franchise record?

2014   When the Cubs took loss No. 10,000 in franchise history on May 11, who did they lose to?

2015   Which team did the Cubs open the season against at home while Wrigley Field was in the midst of extensive renovations?

Answers

1876   The Hartford Dark Blues and St. Louis Brown Stockings.

1877   George Bradley. He had pitched the previous season for St. Louis.

1878   Joe Start

1879   Two, Frank Hankinson and Terry Larkin.

1880   Larry Corcoran and Fred Goldsmith. They combined to go 64–17 and both had an ERA under 2.00.

1881   12 people

1882   35. Outfielder-turned-pitcher Dave Rowe took the loss.

1883   The Boston Beaneaters

1884   Ned Williamson. On May 30, 1884 he became the first player in Major League history to hit three home runs during one game.

1885   Hot Springs, Arkansas

1886   Jim McCormick

1887   John Clarkson

1888   Jimmy Ryan

1889   Bill Hutchison

1890   Bill Hutchison

1891   Hit .300 (.291).

1892   King Kelly, who on the down side of his career played for the Boston Beaneaters that season.

1893   Although the Temple Cup existed, it's false. Chicago finished 56–71, well down the standings.

1894   The book *Green Cathedrals* credits Jimmy Ryan and Walt Wilmot with using bats to get through the fence to save panicked fans.

1895   For "inciting, aiding and abetting the forming of a noisy crowd on a Sunday," Owner Jim Hart posted bail and Chicago pulled out a 13–4 victory.

1896   Ed Delahanty

1897   Bill Lange

1898 Clark Griffith (who was just 5–6, 156 pounds).

1899 The Cleveland Spiders and the Louisville Colonels. Chicago won both games, 13–0 and 7–3, respectively (the second game was called due to darkness after five innings).

1900 Jimmy Ryan

1901 Tom Hughes

1902 Jack Taylor

1903 Jack Doscher. His father Herm Doscher played four seasons in the Major Leagues, including three games with Chicago in 1879.

1904 Frank Chance

1905 Billy Maloney

1906 116. The Cubs went 60–15 on the road, for a .800 winning percentage that has yet to be matched.

1907 When fans started throwing empty bottles at the manager, he threw one back into the crowd and hit a young boy. It sparked a riot.

1908 Orval Overall, who did it in Game 5 of the World Series

1909 Mordecai Brown

1910 King Cole

1911 Jimmy Sheckard

1912 Heinie Zimmerman

1913 Larry Cheney during a 7–0 victory against the New York Giants

1914 Hippo Vaughn with 165

1915 He stole second, third and home, all in the same inning.

1916 Bill Fischer

1917 Because Fred Toney also had a no-hitter going and the game went into extra innings. Hippo Vaughn ended up giving up both a hit and a run in the 10th and the Cubs lost 1–0.

1918 Claude Hendrix (20–7, .741)

1919 Grover Alexander

1920 Max Flack, who batted .302 that season.

1921 Goldie Rapp

1922 Philadelphia Phillies

1923 A riot after umpire Charlie Moran called out Sparky Adams on a controversial play at second base.

1924 Lee Cotter

1925 Broadcasting their regular-season games on the radio.

1926 Hack Wilson

1927 Shortstop Jimmy Cooney. He caught a Paul Waner line drive, stepped on second to retire brother Lloyd Waner and tagged Clyde Barnhart, who was running from first.

1928 Eight double plays in a single game.

1929 Dazzy Vance

1930 Runs. St. Louis scored 1,004 runs to lead the league.

1931 He hit three consecutive home runs to lead a 10–6 victory.

1932 Lon Warneke

1933   An earthquake. Players from both teams had to huddle around the middle of the field until it
       stopped.
1934   He was a starting pitcher and went 11–9 with a 3.91 ERA in his only season with the Cubs.
1935   100 wins.
1936   Four
1937   Augie Galan did it against the Dodgers on June 25.
1938   None of them, which was highly unusual for a team that reached the World Series.
1939   Billy Herman
1940   Stan Hack
1941   An organ.
1942   Merullo's son was born. They named the child Boots. Incidentally, the Cubs still won the
       game, 12–8.
1943   Bill Nicholson
1944   He was the first National League player intentionally walked even though the bases were
       loaded.
1945   Jimmie Foxx. He finished with 534 career home runs.
1946   Claude Passeau
1947   Dom Dallessandro
1948   They were attempting to sign high school players. The Yankees and Phillies were the other
       teams.
1949   Actually, no one did. Johnny Schmitz had the most wins with 11, but had 13 losses.
1950   Ron Northey was the first player to hit three pinch-hit grand slams, although the first two
       were with the St. Louis Cardinals.
1951   Golf legend Sam Snead teed up a ball from home plate and hit the scoreboard as part of a
       pregame publicity stunt before an 8–3 victory against the Cincinnati Reds.
1952   Warren Spahn, who also hit a home run in the game.
1953   Ernie Banks
1954   Dee Fondy
1955   Sam Jones
1956   Most player appearances in a single game (48) and most intentional walks (11).
1957   After teammate Moe Drabowsky was hit by a pitch on his foot Drick Drott got a wheelchair
       and pushed him to first base.
1958   Don Elston
1959   Glen Hobbie
1960   Don Zimmer
1961   12
1962   Houston Colt 45s
1963   Ernie Banks
1964   The St. Louis Cardinals. Incidentally, the first team to do so was the 1923 New York Giants
1965   Jim Maloney of the Cincinnati Reds
1966   Larry Jackson
1967   The New York Mets. The Detroit Tigers and New York Yankees first did it in 1950.
1968   Glenn Beckert

1969 Ernie Banks
1970 The Pittsburgh Pirates
1971 Milt Pappas
1972 Burt Hooten
1973 Glenn Beckert, Don Kessinger, Ron Santo or Randy Hundley. Pitcher Fergie Jenkins was also traded away, but didn't play in that game.
1974 Billy Williams. Carmen Fanzone was second.
1975 Pittsburgh Pirate second baseman Rennis Stennett, had a triple, two doubles, four singles and scored five runs.
1976 Mike Schmidt
1977 Rick Reuschel
1978 45
1979 Dave Kingman
1980 Bill Buckner
1981 Mike Tyson
1982 Gary Templeton
1983 Bill Campbell
1984 Win a title. At 96–65 the Cubs finished atop the National League East.
1985 False, but at $13.478 million they were close, second in the league to the Braves.
1986 Ball girl Marla Collins after she posed nude for *Playboy*. She was 28.
1987 Andre Dawson
1988 The New York Mets.
1989 Mitch Williams
1990 Seven putouts. Over the course of the season he recorded 39 putouts for the year to tie Vic Willis for the National League record set in 1904.
1991 The Pirates rallied back, scoring six runs to win the game and set a record for largest extra-inning comeback.
1992 Commissioner Fay Vincent ordered the realignment of the National League moving the Chicago Cubs and St. Louis Cardinals into the Western Division. However, the owners called for Vincent's resignation and after he obliged the executive council rescinded the realignment.
1993 Tom Browning, who was subsequently fined $500 by Major League Baseball.
1994 Tuffy Rhodes, all off New York Mets pitcher Dwight Gooden.
1995 Mark Grace had 51 doubles while Randy Myers notched 38 saves.
1996 Chan Ho Park of the Los Angeles Dodgers.
1997 Geremi Gonzalez
1998 Steve Trachsel
1999 Jon Lieber, who was 10–11
2000 The Tokyo Dome in Japan, marking the first Major League game ever played on Asian soil. The Cubs beat the Mets, 5–3.
2001 Strikeouts by the pitching staff.
2002 Jon Lieber and Mark Prior.
2003 Sammy Sosa

2004 Greg Maddux

2005 The Philadelphia Phillies, which began as a franchise in 1883 and didn't win a World Series until 1980.

2006 Matt Murton

2007 Carlos Zambrano

2008 Played during the regular season as leaders of their respective divisions.

2009 Ted Lilly (12), Randy Wells (12), and Ryan Dempster (11). Carlos Zambrano and Rich Harden both just missed with nine.

2010 The Chicago White Sox, 3–2, at U.S. Cellular Field.

2011 Starlin Castro

2012 The Houston Astros, who finished 55–107.

2013 50

2014 The Atlanta Braves

2015 The St. Louis Cardinals

Eleven

Drafts, Trades, and Free Agency, Oh My!

It's normal for a Major League Baseball franchise to make numerous personnel moves during a season, and even more during the offseason, but what the Chicago Cubs began in 2011 can only be described as a complete overhaul.

It even included Wrigley Field, which in 2014 began a $575 million, four-year renovation project. Joe Maddon was brought in as manager and the Cubs even ended their longstanding relationship with WGN-AM radio that had dated back to 1925.

On the field the Cubs started building for the future and collecting an impressive group of young players who would hopefully have the team competing at the highest levels for years to follow.

After three straight seasons at the bottom of the National League Central Division, and many people thought the young team was still a year away from seriously challenging for a playoff spot, the Cubs advanced to the NL Championship Series in 2015 while the changes continued.

Drafts, Trades, and Free Agency

1. Who was the first player selected by the Cubs in the inaugural First-Year Player Draft in 1965?
2. Which future Cub was the first player selected in that draft?
3. Through 2015 how many draft picks by the Cubs had been enshrined in the Hall of Fame?
4. Which first-round draft pick won the Major League Rookie of the Year award?
5. Who did the Cubs select the only time they had the first-overall selection in the draft?
6. How was Henry Borowy, who proceeded to win eleven of thirteen decisions and helped Chicago fight off the St. Louis Cardinals in the National League pennant race, acquired in 1945?
7. From which rival did Chicago acquire Mordecai Brown in 1903?
8. Name any of the players involved in the deal when the Cubs traded away Joe Tinker in 1912.
9. Whom did the Cubs acquire from the Pirates for Sparky Adams and Pete Scott on November 27, 1927?
10. On the eve of the 1960 World Series, Joe Reichler of the Associated Press reported that the Milwaukee Braves were prepared to pay cash and trade pitchers Joey Jay, Carlton Willey and Don Nottebart, outfielder Billy Bruton, shortstop Johnny Logan and first baseman Frank Torre to the Cubs for which player?
11. What trade does every Cubs fan wish had never happened?
12. What future Hall of Fame pitcher did the Cubs acquire from the Philadelphia Phillies on April 21, 1966?
13. Who did the Cubs sign to a free-agent deal in 1997 after he had hit .351 with 15 home runs and 48 RBIs against them in 299 at-bats?

14. Which Japanese player did the Cubs sign to a four-year contract for $48 million?

15. Who did the Cubs sign to a three-year deal for $30 million in 2009, only to trade him away after one season?

16. Who did the Cubs trade to Oakland on October 23, 1974 in exchange for infielder Manny Trillo and pitchers Darold Knowles and Bob Locker?

17. On January 27, 1982, who was the player the Phillies threw in to complete the Larry Bowa for Ivan DeJesus trade?

18. Which Hall of Fame pitcher did the Cubs acquire in exchange for Bill Buckner on May 25, 1984?

19. Name everyone in the seven-player deal between the Cubs and Indians on June 13, 1984.

20. Who did the Cubs send to the Chicago White Sox in exchange for Sammy Sosa on March 30, 1992?

Answers

1. Right-handed pitcher Rick James. He played in three games in the Major Leagues, and just 4⅔ innings.
2. Rick Monday by the Kansas City Athletics
3. None
4. Kerry Wood in 1995.
5. Shawon Dunston
6. The Cubs bought his rights from the New York Yankees for approximately $97,000. Larry MacPhail was quoted as saying: "This was a good chance to sell a pitcher who never has been a winner in the last month or so of a season."
7. The St. Louis Cardinals on December 3, 1903. The trade was Mordecai Brown and Jack O'Neill for Larry McLean and Jack Taylor.
8. Joe Tinker, Harry Chapman and Grover Lowdermilk went to the Reds in exchange for Red Corriden, Bert Humphries, Pete Knisely, Mike Mitchell and Art Phelan.
9. Kiki Cuyler
10. Ernie Banks. Obviously the trade never happened.
11. The Cubs traded away Lou Brock to rival St. Louis on June 15, 1964. The six-player deal was Brock, Jack Spring, and Paul Toth for Ernie Broglio, Bobby Shantz, and Doug Clemens.
12. Ferguson Jenkins. The deal was Jenkins, John Herrnstein and Adolfo Phillips from the Phillies for Bob Buhl and Larry Jackson.
13. Jeff Blauser

14. Kosuke Fukudome
15. Milton Bradley
16. Billy Williams
17. Ryne Sandberg
18. Dennis Eckersley. Mike Brumley was also part of the trade with the Boston Red Sox.
19. The Cubs acquired Rick Sutcliffe, George Frazier and Ron Hassey from the Indians for Joe Carter, Mel Hall, Don Schultze and Darryl Banks.
20. George Bell

Twelve

Opening Day Lineups

When it comes to baseball trivia there's nothing like an Opening Day lineup.

It's when the newest players first appear, departures become more real and the changes over the offseason take hold. Among pitchers it's when the staff ace usually takes his rightful place and begins what's hopefully the long march toward the playoffs.

For some reason fans can remember and recite Opening Day lineups until their dying day even though it could look different with each passing game. More than an annual benchmark, it's like a progress report, and no one ever remembers who started the second game of a 162-game season.

Opening Day Lineups

See how many of these 25 seasons you can peg the Opening Day lineup:

1. 1876
2. 1885
3. 1907
4. 1910
5. 1918
6. 1924
7. 1929
8. 1932
9. 1935
10. 1938
11. 1945
12. 1948
13. 1954
14. 1960
15. 1966
16. 1972
17. 1978
18. 1984
19. 1989
20. 1998
21. 2003
22. 2007
23. 2008
24. 2011
25. 2015

Anthony Rizzo takes a photo of the falling snow during Opening Day 2013. (Gene J. Puskar)

Answers

1. **1876**
   Ross Barnes 2B
   Cap Anson 3B
   Calvin McVey 1B
   Paul Hines CF
   Albert Spaulding P
   Bob Addy RF
   Deacon White C
   Johnny Peters SS
   John Glenn LF

2. **1885**
   Abner Dalrymple LF
   George Gore CF
   King Kelly RF
   Cap Anson 1B
   Fred Pfeffer 2B
   Ned Williamson 3B
   Tom Burns SS
   Larry Corcoran P
   Silver Flint C

3. **1907**
   Jimmy Slagle CF
   Jimmy Sheckard LF
   Wildfire Schulte RF
   Frank Chance 1B
   Harry Steinfeldt 3B
   Solly Hofman SS
   Johnny Evers 2B
   Pat Moran C
   Orval Overall P

4. **1910**
   Johnny Evers 2B
   Ginger Beaumont LF
   Wildfire Schulte RF
   Frank Chance 1B
   Harry Steinfeldt 3B
   Solly Hofman CF
   Joe Tinker SS
   Jimmy Archer C
   Orval Overall P

5. **1918**
   Charlie Hollocher SS
   Max Flack RF
   Les Mann LF
   Dode Paskert CF
   Fred Merkle 1B
   Pete Kilduff 2B
   Charlie Deal 3B
   Bill Killefer C
   Grover Alexander P

6. **1924**
   Jigger Statz CF
   Sparky Adams SS
   George Grantham 2B
   Ray Grimes 1B
   Barney Friberg 3B
   Hack Miller LF
   Otto Vogel RF
   Bob O'Farrell C
   Vic Aldridge P

7. **1929**
   Woody English SS
   Clyde Beck 3B
   Kiki Cuyler RF
   Rogers Hornsby 2B
   Hack Wilson CF
   Riggs Stephenson LF
   Charlie Grimm 1B
   Mike Gonzalez C
   Charlie Root P

8. **1932**
   Stan Hack 3B
   Billy Herman 2B
   Kiki Cuyler CF
   Vince Barton RF
   Riggs Stephenson LF
   Gabby Hartnett C
   Charlie Grimm 1B
   Billy Jurges SS
   Charlie Root P

9. **1935**
Augie Galan LF
Billy Herman 2B
Kiki Cuyler CF
Freddie Lindstrom 3B
Chuck Klein RF
Charlie Grimm 1B
Gabby Hartnett C
Billy Jurges SS
Lon Warneke P

10. **1938**
Stan Hack 3B
Billy Herman 2B
Ripper Collins 1B
Frank Demaree RF
Joe Marty CF
Coaker Triplett LF
Billy Jurges SS
Gabby Hartnett C
Clay Bryant P

11. **1945**
Stan Hack 3B
Lennie Merullo SS
Phil Cavarretta 1B
Bill Nicholson RF
Ed Sauer LF
Andy Pafko CF
Don Johnson 2B
Mickey Livingston C
Paul Derringer P

12. **1948**
Hank Schenz 2B
Eddie Waitkus 1B
Hal Jeffcoat CF
Andy Pafko 3B
Phil Cavarretta LF
Bill Nicholson RF
Clyde McCullough C
Roy Smalley SS
Russ Meyer P

13. **1954**
Bobby Talbot CF
Dee Fondy 1B
Ralph Kiner LF
Hank Sauer RF
Randy Jackson 3B
Ernie Banks SS
Gene Baker 2B
Clyde McCullough C
Paul Minner P

14. **1960**
Richie Ashburn CF
Tony Taylor 2B
Bob Will RF
Ernie Banks SS
Frank Thomas LF
George Altman 1B
Don Zimmer 3B
Cal Neeman C
Bob Anderson P

15. **1966**
Ty Cline CF
Glenn Beckert 2B
Billy Williams RF
Ron Santo 3B
George Altman LF
Ernie Banks 1B
Randy Hundley C
Don Kessinger SS
Larry Jackson P

16. **1972**
Jose Cardenal RF
Glenn Beckert 2B
Billy Williams LF
Ron Santo 3B
Joe Pepitone 1B
Randy Hundley C
Rick Monday CF
Don Kessinger SS
Fergie Jenkins P

17. **1978**
    Ivan DeJesus SS
    Gene Clines CF
    Bill Buckner 1B
    Bobby Murcer RF
    Dave Kingman LF
    Steve Ontiveros 3B
    Manny Trillo 2B
    Dave Rader C
    Rick Reuschel P
18. **1984**
    Bobby Dernier CF
    Ryne Sandberg 2B
    Gary Matthews LF
    Ron Cey 3B
    Keith Moreland RF
    Jody Davis C
    Leon Durham 1B
    Larry Bowa SS
    Dick Ruthven P
19. **1989**
    Jerome Walton CF
    Mitch Webster LF
    Ryne Sandberg 2B
    Andre Dawson RF
    Mark Grace 1B
    Vance Law 3B
    Shawon Dunston SS
    Joe Girardi C
    Rick Sutcliffe P
20. **1998**
    Lance Johnson CF
    Mickey Morandini 2B
    Sammy Sosa RF
    Mark Grace 1B
    Henry Rodriguez LF
    Jeff Blauser 22
    Kevin Orie 3B
    Scott Servais C
    Kevin Tapani P

21. **2003**
    Mark Grudzielanek 2B
    Alex Gonzalez SS
    Sammy Sosa RF
    Moises Alou LF
    Hee-Seop Choi 1B
    Mark Bellhorn 3B
    Corey Patterson CF
    Damian Miller C
    Kerry Wood P
22. **2007**
    Alfonso Soriano CF
    Matt Murton LF
    Derrek Lee 1B
    Aramis Ramirez 3B
    Jacque Jones RF
    Michael Barrett C
    Mark DeRosa 2B
    Cesar Izturis SS
    Carlos Zambrano P
23. **2008**
    Ryan Theriot SS
    Alfonso Soriano LF
    Derrek Lee 1B
    Aramis Ramirez 3B
    Kosuke Fukudome RF
    Mark DeRosa 2B
    Geovany Soto C
    Felix Pie CF
    Carlos Zambrano P
24. **2011**
    Kosuke Fukudome RF
    Starlin Castro SS
    Marlon Byrd CF
    Aramis Ramirez 3B
    Carlos Peña 1B
    Geovany Soto C
    Alfonso Soriano LF
    Darwin Barney 2B
    Ryan Dempster P

25. 2015
Dexter Fowler CF
Jorge Soler RF
Anthony Rizzo 1B
Starlin Castro SS
Chris Coghlan LF
Mike Olt 3B
David Ross C
John Lester P
Tommy LaStella 2B

The Postseason

 1885

1. True or false, the 1885 World Series is considered the first recognized by Major League Baseball.
2. What team did Chicago face?
3. In what four cities was the series played?
4. Who won the series?
5. What's at the heart of the dispute?
6. What was done to try to resolve it?
7. Which pitcher started five of the games in the series for Chicago?
8. Who was the only other Chicago player to pitch in the series?
9. Which Chicago player batted .423 in the series?
10. Who had led the team with a .313 batting average during the regular season?

Answers

1. False. The series was dubbed the World's Championship between the top teams of the National League and the American Association. The American League as we know it now didn't exist yet.
2. The St. Louis Browns, who are now known as the St. Louis Cardinals.
3. Chicago, St. Louis, Pittsburgh and Cincinnati.
4. Depends on whom you ask. Most consider it a 3–3–1 tie and, perhaps most importantly, the teams split the money at the end of the series.
5. During Game 2, Browns manager Charles Comiskey called his team off the field to protest a ruling made by umpire Dave Sullivan. The game was forfeited to Chicago, which was ahead at the time 5–4 in the sixth inning. The Browns allegedly claimed the forfeit shouldn't count as a loss.
6. A special committee was formed to try and determine a winner, but it could not.
7. Jim McCormick
8. John Clarkson
9. Cap Anson
10. George Gore

1886

1. Who did Chicago face from the American Association?
2. How was the series promoted?
3. In how many consecutive days was the series played?
4. Which team won?
5. Who threw a five-hit shutout for Chicago in Game 1?
6. Who was the first player to hit two home runs in a postseason game?
7. Which two position players ended up pitching for Chicago in Game 5?
8. How did the winning run score in Game 6?
9. What was the play dubbed?
10. In terms of bragging rights between the National League and American Association, why was the outcome important?

Answers

1. The St. Louis Browns in a rematch of the 1885 championship.
2. As a best-of-seven winner-takes-all of the prize money after the previous matchup essentially ended in a tie.
3. Six.
4. The Browns
5. Jim Clarkson
6. Tip O'Neill of the Browns in Game 2, a 12–0 victory for St. Louis.
7. Shortstop Ned Williamson and outfielder Jimmy Ryan after Jim Clarkson started three of the first four games.
8. With one out in the bottom of the tenth inning and St Louis' Curt Welch on third base Chicago's Clarkson threw a pitch that got past catcher King Kelly.
9. The "$15,000 slide," although St. Louis only received $13,920 in prize money. It was also called the most famous play in 19ᵗʰ-century baseball.
10. It was the American Association's only non-disputed championship over the National League.

1906

1. How many regular-season games did the Cubs win to set a "modern" single-season record?
2. Who did the Cubs face in the World Series and what famous first was that matchup?
3. What was that team nicknamed by the local media before the series?
4. What was the Cubs' team ERA during the regular season?
5. Despite that, what was the outcome of the series?
6. Who won both games he started, allowed just seven hits and struck 17 batters over 15 innings while posting a 1.20 ERA?
7. How many home runs were hit in the series?
8. Who was the Cubs' best hitter in the series with a .304 average?
9. Who were the only two Cubs to take a loss in the series?
10. True or false, the losing team in the series tallied more runs and hits than the winning team.

Answers

1. 116
2. The Chicago White Sox, in the first World Series between two teams from the same city.
3. The Hitless Wonders after hitting .230 as a team during the regular season.
4. 1.76
5. The White Sox won in six games.
6. Ed Walsh
7. None.
8. Center fielder Solly Hofman, who had appeared in only 64 games during the regular season.
9. Mordecai Brown and Jack Pfiester.
10. False. The Cubs were outscored 22–18, and outhit 37–36. But the White Sox had a .198 team batting average in the series and the Cubs hit .196.

1907

1. Who did the Cubs face in the World Series?
2. What was the outcome?
3. How many games did the two teams play and why?
4. During their victories how many total runs did the Cubs give up?
5. Who, at the age of 20, came into the series having led the American League in hits, runs batted in, batting average, slugging percentage and stolen bases?
6. What did he bat in the series?
7. Which notable person batted .214 and scored three runs for the Cubs?
8. Who led the Cubs in stolen bases in the series?
9. Out of the 48 innings played in the series in how many did the Cubs give up a run?
10. For the second straight year an opposing pitcher struck out 12 Cubs in a World Series game. Who was it?
11. Which Chicago pitcher scattered 10 hits, but allowed just one run in Game 2?
12. How did the Cubs score their first run of Game 2?
13. Who then followed with a similar result, albeit with six hits, in Game 3?
14. Who subsequently topped both of them by allowing just five hits in Game 4?
15. Who had a two-run single to right to give the Cubs the lead in the fifth inning?
16. What was unusual about the Cubs' three-run rally in the seventh inning of Game 4?
17. Who threw a seven-hit shutout to close out the series?
18. Who had seven hits over the last three games and batted .471 for the series (8-for-17)?
19. Who had seven hits over the first three games and batted .350 for the series (7-for-20)?
20. Which number was greater, the number of runs the Cubs gave up, or the number of errors its opponent made?

Answers

1. The Detroit Tigers.
2. The Cubs won the series 4–0.
3. They actually played five games, with Game 1 called due to darkness after 12 innings with the score tied 3–3.
4. Three
5. Ty Cobb
6. .200. He was 4-for-20 with a triple, one run scored and three strikeouts.
7. Frank Chance, who played first base and also managed the Cubs.
8. Jimmy Slagle with six. Overall, the Cubs went crazy on the basepaths, stealing 18 bases.
9. Five. The Cubs' staff ERA was 0.75.
10. Wild Bill Donovan, although he needed 12 innings to do so in Game 1.
11. Jack Pfiester
12. George Mullin issued a bases-loaded walk.
13. Ed Reulbach
14. Orval Overall
15. Orval Overall
16. The ball never left the infield. The Cubs dropped down four bunts, two for hits.
17. Mordecai Brown
18. Harry Steinfeldt
19. Johnny Evers
20. The errors. The Tigers scored six runs and made nine errors.

1908

1. What first in the young history of the World Series occurred with the matchup?
2. Which team clinched its respective pennant first?
3. Why did the Cubs and Giants play an extra game on Oct. 8?
4. What first in how the games were called occurred during the series?
5. How close were the Cubs to losing Game 1 when they strung together six straight hits?
6. Who threw a complete game for the Cubs in Game 2 after serving as a reliever in Game 1?
7. Who hit the first home run in World Series history during Game 2?
8. What did the Cubs do for the only time during the 1907 and 1908 World Series in Game 3?
9. Who had a monster game, but was thrown out trying to steal home?
10. Who were the winning and losing pitchers?
11. Who threw a pitching gem in Game 4, allowing just four hits while notching a shutout?
12. Who had RBI singles in the third inning to give the Cubs the lead?
13. How long did it take to play Game 4?
14. Who topped the pitching performance in Game 5?
15. What unusual first did he record in World Series history?
16. In what way was Game 5 considered perfect?
17. Who led both teams with eight hits and batted .421 in the series?
18. What pitcher finished the series without having yielded a run?
19. What World Series "low" was set and still stands?
20. What scandal had a negative impact on that?

Answers

1. It was the first rematch of the previous year's series, the Chicago Cubs vs. the Detroit Tigers.
2. The Tigers did by winning on the last day of the regular season, Oct. 6, to edge the Cleveland Naps by a half-game in the American League standings.
3. The makeup game to determine the pennant was ordered after what's been described "the most controversial game in baseball history," "Merkle's Boner." Specifically, when 19-year-old Fred Merkle didn't touch second base on what should have been a game-winning hit he was called out as Giants fans stormed the field celebrating the win. Because umpires couldn't clear the field to resume play the game was eventually called due to darkness with a 1–1 tie, resulting in the winner-takes-all makeup game between the Cubs and Giants.
4. For the first time four umpires were used, in alternating two-man teams.
5. Two outs, they had one out in the ninth inning when the six hits resulted in five runs.
6. Orval Overall
7. Joe Tinker
8. Lose, 8–3.
9. Ty Cobb. He went 4-for-5 with a double and two stolen bases. He was 21 at the time.
10. George Mullin got the win, Jack Pfiester took the loss.
11. Mordecai Brown
12. Harry Steinfeldt and Solly Hofman.
13. Just 95 minutes.
14. Orval Overall, who threw a three-hit shutout.
15. He was the first pitcher to strike out four batters in one inning. He did it in the first inning.
16. It was the first World Series game played without either side committing an error.
17. Cubs player-manager Frank Chance.
18. Mordecai Brown, who went 2–0 with a 0.00 ERA.
19. Only 6,210 fans were in attendance for the final game.
20. The owner of the Cubs was accused of being involved in a ticket-scalping scheme. Overall, the total attendance was 62,232, for an average of 12,446.

1910

1. Even though the Cubs won 104 games in 1909, which team edged them in the standings and kept them from appearing in five straight World Series?
2. After three straight World Series appearances by the Detroit Tigers, which team won the American League pennant?
3. Which team had won more games during the regular season?
4. What pitcher won three games in the series?
5. How many games did he win during the regular season?
6. Who threw a three-hitter, with eight strikeouts, to set the tone in Game 1?
7. What World Series offensive first occurred during Game 2?
8. Who hit a ninth-inning triple to send Game 4 into extra innings?
9. Who knocked in the winning run with two outs in the 10th inning to keep the series from being a sweep?
10. Who became the first player in World Series history to appear for both a National and American league team when he participated in Game 3?

1918

1. Why was the Fall Classic played in early September?

2. Where did the Cubs play their home games in the World Series?

3. What tradition was first observed during Game 1?

4. In Game 1, who extended his postseason scoreless innings streak from 13 to 22 while earning the win?

5. Who gave up just six hits while getting the win in Game 2?

6. Who threw 27 innings in the series and gave up just three runs, for a 1.00 ERA, but went 1–2?

7. Which team had a better batting average in the series?

8. What would happen first, the two teams in the 1918 World Series would play again or one of the teams would win another World Series?

9. The 1918 World Series was the last one to not include what?

10. The threat of what loomed over the series and fed accusations later on that were never proven?

Answers

1. The regular season was shortened and ended on Labor Day due to World War I.
2. Comiskey Park due to its larger seating capacity.
3. The "Star Spangled Banner" was performed for the first time at a Major League game. It was played during the seventh inning and would be declared the national anthem in 1931.
4. Babe Ruth
5. Lefty Tyler
6. Hippo Vaughn
7. The Cubs, even though they hit a horrendous .210 in the series. The Red Sox batted just .186 while winning in six games.
8. The teams wouldn't meet again for 87 years, until 2005, one year after the Red Sox broke the "Curse of the Bambino" by winning the 2004 World Series.
9. A home run. The only other three to not have at least one were played in 1905, 1906 and 1907.
10. A player's strike due to low gate receipts. During the investigation of the 1919 Black Sox Scandal it was alleged that the Cubs threw the series to make up for their financial losses.

1929

1. Although the Cubs had been in the World Series numerous times, what first occurred with Game 1?

2. Why did Connie Mack put prized starters Lefty Grove and Rube Walberg in the bullpen for the series?

3. Who was the surprise starter of Game 1 for the A's?

4. What advantage did the stadium provide that pitcher?

5. Who was the first player to hit a home run in his first two World Series games?

6. Who won a pitcher's duel in Game 3 for the Cubs?

7. Who was Connie Mack's surprise starter in Game 4?

8. What is commonly referred to as the "Mack Attack"?

9. In the middle of that rally, who lost Mule Haas' fly ball in the sun for a three-run inside-the-park home run? (Bonus: In what song is it immortalized?)

10. Who hit the walk-off double in Game 5 to clinch the series for the A's?

Answers

1. It was the first World Series game played at Wrigley Field.
2. Because seven of the eight Cubs regulars were right-handed, he only started two right-handed pitchers.
3. Howard Ehmke, who was 7–2 with a 3.29 ERA during the regular season. During the stretch run he had Ehmke anonymously attend Cubs games to scout them. He struck out 13 batters to set a World Series record and the A's won 3–1.
4. Ehmke had a sidearm delivery, which combined with the fans wearing white shirts in the famous Wrigley Field bleachers made it harder for the batters to pick up the ball coming out of the pitcher's hand.
5. Jimmie Foxx in Game 1 and Game 2.
6. Guy Bush out-pitched George Earnshaw for the 3–1 victory.
7. 46-year-old Jack Quinn. This time it backfired as he gave up seven runs in six innings.
8. Down 8–0, the A's rallied for 10 runs in the seventh inning.
9. Hack Wilson. The song My Old Kentucky Home begins with "The sun shone bright into poor Hack Wilson's eyes...."
10. Bing Miller.

Lou Gehrig crosses home plate behind Babe Ruth after hitting a three-run homer in Game 1 of the 1932 World Series against the Cubs.

1932

1. Why were the teams verbally attacking each other in the press before the series even started?
2. Who was the manager of the New York Yankees?
3. Who started Game 1 for the Cubs, and in two appearances had a 14.29 ERA due to nine earned runs allowed?
4. Who made his final World Series appearance at Yankee Stadium in Game 2?
5. What hotly debated and widely contested moment highlighted Game 3?
6. Which opposing player hit two two-run home runs to lead a 13–6 victory in Game 4?
7. Who hit .444 (8-for-18) in the losing effort?
8. Who hit .592 (9-for-17), with three home runs, nine runs and eight RBIs to lead the winning effort?
9. Who said: "If he had (called his home run), I would have knocked him down with the next pitch"?
10. Who was in the on-deck circle when Ruth supposedly called his shot?

Answers

1. The Cubs had voted that shortstop Mark Koenig, who had hit .353 for the team, should receive only half a player's postseason share of any winnings because he had only played in 33 games and was sidelined for the World Series due to injury. Things quickly escalated.
2. Former Cubs manager Joe McCarthy, who had been fired after the 1930 season.
3. Guy Bush
4. Babe Ruth
5. Babe Ruth allegedly called his shot before hitting a home run to break a 4–4 tie at Wrigley Field.
6. Tony Lazzeri
7. Riggs Stephenson
8. Lou Gehrig
9. Pitcher Charlie Root
10. Lou Gehrig

1935

1. How many consecutive games did the Cubs win in September to claim the pennant?

2. Which opponent did the Cubs face for the third time in the World Series?

3. Who threw a four-hit shutout for the Cubs in Game 1?

4. Which player suffered a broken wrist while trying to score in Game 2?

5. Which two moves did his absence lead to?

6. Who had lost Game 1 and had a blown save in Game 3, only to get the win in extra innings?

7. What hometown first did the Cubs pull off in Game 5?

8. Who led off the ninth inning of Game 6 with a triple, only to be left stranded in the 4–3 loss?

9. Who at the age of 19 became the youngest Cub to participate in postseason play?

10. Combined with other results, what was Detroit dubbed in 1935–36?

Answers

1. 21
2. The Detroit Tigers, who won in six games.
3. Lon Warneke
4. Hank Greenberg
5. Detroit switched third baseman Marv Owen to first in Greenberg's spot, and inserted Flea Clifton at third. They combined to go 1-for-36 the rest of the series.
6. Schoolboy Rowe
7. It was their first World Series victory at Wrigley Field.
8. Stan Hack
9. Phil Cavarretta
10. The City of Champions. In addition to the Tigers winning their first World Series, the Lions won the 1935 NFL Championship Game, followed by the Detroit Red Wings capturing the 1935–36 Stanley Cup. Joe Louis also won the heavyweight boxing championship.

1938

1. With a 6–5 ninth-inning win on September 28ᵗʰ who did the Cubs move past in the standings and hold off to capture the pennant?

2. Who started Games 1 and 4 and won them both despite giving up 17 hits?

3. Who started Games 1 and 4 and lost them both despite walking just one batter?

4. Who went 4-for-4 for the New York Yankees to lead the 3–1 victory in Game 1?

5. Who had the fewest home runs of the Yankees regulars during the season, but hit the key two-run home run in the eighth inning of Game 2?

6. Which better-known Yankee added a two-run home run of his own in the ninth inning?

7. Whose "last stand" was Game 2?

8. Whose home run in the sixth inning of Game 4 ended up scoring the game-winning run?

9. With the win, what did the Yankees become the first team to do in Major League history?

10. Which notable Yankee made his last World Series appearance in Game 4?

1945

1. Which familiar World Series opponent did the Cubs face?
2. Who had been discharged from military service and hit his team's only two home runs in the series?
3. Which starting pitcher did the Cubs pound in Game 1?
4. Who gave up just one run while going the distance in Game 2 to even the series?
5. Who threw a one-hitter for the Cubs in Game 3?
6. Who had the lone hit and in what inning?
7. Who countered with a complete-game win in Game 4?
8. Who was the winning pitcher in Game 1 and 6, but was the losing pitcher in Game 5?
9. Who described the 12-inning Game 6, which featured 28 hits, four errors and nine pitchers, as "the worst game of baseball ever played in this country"?
10. Who started and took the loss in Game 7?

Answers
1. The Detroit Tigers, who were 1–5 in the Fall Classic with their only win coming against the 1935 Cubs.
2. Hank Greenberg
3. Hal Newhouser, who had won 25 games during the regular season.
4. Virgil Trucks
5. Claude Passeau
6. Rudy York in the second inning
7. Dizzy Trout
8. Hank Borowy
9. Sportswriter, author and baseball historian Charles Einstein.
10. Hank Borowy, who lasted three batters, who all singled, as the Tigers rallied for five runs en route to a 9–3 victory.

1984

1. True or false, the Cubs were deprived of home-field advantage in the National League Championship Series against San Diego because Wrigley Field didn't have lights and thus couldn't host a night game.

2. Who led off Game 1 with a home run for the Cubs?

3. What was the final score of Game 1?

4. Who notched the win in Game 2 to put the Cubs one win away from the World Series?

5. Which future Hall of Famer was the losing pitcher in Game 3?

6. Who hit home runs in the fourth inning of Game 4 to give the Cubs the lead?

7. Who hit a two-run home run in the ninth inning, giving him five RBIs, to force a winner-takes-all game?

8. Who hit home runs in the first two innings of Game 5 to give the Cubs the lead?

9. Before Game 5, what was Rick Sutcliffe's record with the Cubs since being acquired in a June trade?

10. What major format change occurred with the subsequent season?

Answers

1. False. While it's true that Wrigley Field didn't have lights, at the time the League Championship Series were best-of-5, played in a 2–3 format.
2. Bob Dernier
3. 13–0
4. Steve Trout
5. Dennis Eckersley
6. Jody Davis and Leon Durham
7. Steve Garvey
8. Leon Durham and Jody Davis
9. 17–1
10. The League Championship Series changed to a best-of-seven format in 1985.

Rick Sutcliffe watches his home run fly out of Wrigley Field during Game 1 of the 1984 NLCS. (John Swart)

1989

1. True or false, the Cubs beat out the New York Mets for the National League East title despite having just over half of their payroll.
2. Which future Hall of Famer was the losing pitcher in Game 1?
3. Who, thanks to a grand slam, needed just four innings to tie the National League Championship Series record for RBIs in a series?
4. How many RBIs did he finish with in the series while batting .650?
5. Which starting pitcher did the Cubs chase during a six-run first inning en route to a 9–5 victory in Game 2?
6. Who hit the key home run in the seventh inning of Game 3 for the Giants?
7. Who hit an early home run for the Cubs in Game 4, only to see the lead not hold up?
8. Who made the final out after the Cubs notched three straight hits to pull within 3–2 in the ninth inning?
9. Who went 11-for-17 (.647) with five extra-base hits and eight RBIs for the Cubs?
10. Sadly, who broke his pitching arm during the victory celebration and would eventually have his it amputated due to cancer?

1998

1. Who did the Cubs have to defeat in a playoff game to secure the National League wild-card spot?
2. Who was the winning pitcher in that game?
3. Which team did the Cubs face in the National League Divisional Series, and how many more wins did that team have during the regular season?
4. Who hit a grand slam during Game 1?
5. How did the Cubs score their only run?
6. The Game 2 pitching matchup was a rematch from the 1991 World Series. Who started for each team?
7. Who ended up taking the loss in the 10th inning?
8. Who became the youngest pitcher in franchise history to see action in the postseason when he started Game 3?
9. Who hit a grand slam in the eighth inning to essentially end the series?
10. Who was the winning pitcher?

2003

1. Which team did the Cubs squeak by to win the National League Central Division by one game?
2. Why did the Cubs draw the top-seeded Atlanta Braves in the National League Division Series instead of the wild-card team?
3. Who doubled in two runs and then scored what would be the game-winning run in the sixth inning of Game 1?
4. Which opposing pitcher struck out six straight batters to tie a Major League postseason record? (Bonus: Name the three pitchers he tied.)
5. Who hit a two-out, two-run double in the eighth inning to tie up the series?
6. Who threw a two-hitter to top Greg Maddux in his last start for the Atlanta Braves in Game 3?
7. Who hit two home runs for the Cubs in a losing effort in Game 4?
8. Who was the first Cubs pitcher to notch two wins in a postseason series since Hank Borowy in the 1945 World Series?
9. How many errors did the Cubs make in the NL Division Series?
10. Which team did the Cubs face in the National League Championship Series?
11. What movie sort of predicted that the Cubs would face a team from Miami in the 2015 World Series?
12. Who hit the game-winning home run in the 11th inning of Game 1?
13. Who hit two home runs to pace the Cubs' 12–3 victory in Game 2?
14. In the top of the 11th inning, who tripled to score Kenny Lofton for what would be the winning run of Game 3?
15. Who hit the first grand slam in Cubs postseason history in the first inning of Game 4?
16. Who gave up just two hits while getting the win in Game 5?
17. With a 3–0 lead in Game 6, how many outs were the Cubs from the World Series when the Marlins rallied for eight runs?

18. Who hit home runs to give the Cubs a 5–3 lead in Game 7?
19. Which team scored more runs in the series and which team had more hits?
20. Who fell short in his bid to become the first manager ever to take different teams to the World Series in consecutive years?

Sammy Sosa does his trademark hop after connecting on a two-run homer in Game 2 of the 2003 NLCS. (Paul Sancya)

Answers

1. The Houston Astros
2. Although the team with the best record would normally play the wild-card team, the Braves played the Cubs, rather than the wild-card Marlins, because the Braves and Marlins are in the same division.
3. Kerry Wood, who was the starting pitcher
4. **Mike Hampton.** He tied Todd Worrell in 1985, Moe Drabowski in 1966 and Hod Eller in 1919.
5. **Mark DeRosa**
6. **Mark Prior.** He was the first Cubs pitcher to throw a complete game in the postseason since Claude Passeau in Game 3 of the 1945 World Series.
7. Eric Karros
8. Kerry Wood, who was the winning pitcher in Games 1 and 5
9. Zero
10. The Florida Marlins
11. *Back to the Future II*, which was made before the Marlins existed.
12. Florida pinch-hitter Mike Lowell.
13. Alex S. Gonzalez, not to be mistaken with the Marlins' Alex L. Gonzalez,
14. Doug Glanville
15. Aramis Ramirez
16. Josh Beckett
17. Five
18. Kerry Wood and Moises Alou.
19. The Cubs scored more runs 42–40, but the Marlins had more hits 68–65.
20. Dusty Baker

2007

1. How many more games in the regular season did the Cubs win compared to 2006?

2. Which team did the Cubs edge to win the National League Central Division?

3. Despite being the top-seeded team in the National League playoffs what statistical aberration did the Arizona Diamondbacks have for a division winning team?

4. Which Cubs reliever took the loss in Game 1?

5. Which starter was outpitched by Doug Davis in Game 2?

6. How many hits did the Cubs have with men in scoring position?

7. How many runs did the Cubs score in the series?

8. Who hit the Cubs' only home run?

9. True or false: The home run was the only time the Cubs had a lead during the series.

10. Before him who was the only Cubs rookie to hit a home run in postseason play?

2008

1. True or false: After notching 97 wins during the regular season the Cubs were the top-seeded team in the National League playoffs.
2. Who issued a career-high seven walks and took the loss in Game 1?
3. Who hit a grand slam for the Dodgers to pace the 7–2 victory?
4. What Cubs starting pitcher struggled in Game 2?
5. True or false: Each Cubs starting infielder made an error as the Dodgers scored five unearned runs, including four in the five-run second inning.
6. Who took third on a single by Manny Ramírez in the bottom of the first inning of Game 3, and in a controversial ruling was called safe (when replays showed he appeared to be out)?
7. Who subsequently doubled in both players with the second run holding up as the game winner?
8. Whose pinch-hit single scored the Cubs only run in Game 3?
9. Who took the loss in Game 3?
10. True or false: Despite scoring just six runs the Cubs outhit the Dodgers in the series.

Fans gather on the streets outside of Wrigley Field after the Cubs beat the Cardinals in Game 4 of the 2015 NLDS to sweep the series. (Paul Beaty)

2015

1. Who was the first Cubs pitcher to throw a postseason shutout since Claude Passeau in the 1945 World Series?

2. Who said after the game that the pitch count for the Cubs' starter was "infinity."

3. Who got outpitched by a former teammate on a World Series winning team in Game 1 of the National League Division Series?

4. Who hit a two-run home run to highlight a five-run second inning in Game 2?

5. How many home runs did the Cubs hit in Game 3 to set a postseason record? (Bonus: Name the players who hit them.)

6. What did the Cubs do for the first time in franchise history on October 13, 2015?

7. Why did the Cubs decide to leave the home run ball hit by Kyle Schwarber in Game 4 where it was for the duration of the playoffs?

8. True or false, no batted ball has ever hit the center field scoreboard during a game at Wrigley Field.

9. Who gave up four hits while striking out nine batters over 7⅔ innings to get the win in Game 1 of the National League Championship Series?

10. In Game 2, who gave up his first first-inning run in 25 consecutive starts dating back to May 29?

11. Who hit his fifth postseason home run in the first inning of Game 3?

12. In Game 4, who set a record by hitting a home run in his sixth consecutive postseason game?

13. Who set a Major League record for longest amount of time between postseason victories?

14. Tue or false, the Cubs never had a lead in the series.

15. What was the Mets' record against the Cubs during the regular season?

Answers

1. Jake Arrieta in the single-elimination wild-card game against Pittsburgh. He gave up just four hits in the 4–0 victory.
2. Manager Joe Maddon
3. Jon Lester was outdueled by John Lackey of the St. Louis Cardinals. They were teammates on the 2013 champion Boston Red Sox.
4. Jorge Soler
5. Six, one each by Jorge Soler, Kris Bryant, Kyle Schwarber, Starlin Castro, Anthony Rizzo and Dexter Fowler.
6. Clinch a postseason series at Wrigley Field.
7. It was the first ball that landed on top of the right-field video scoreboard that had been installed before the start of the season. It was encased in Plexiglas to protect it, though.
8. True. Two came very close, a home run by Bill Nicholson that landed on Sheffield Avenue in 1948, and one hit by Roberto Clemente onto Waveland Avenue in 1959.
9. Matt Harvey of the New York Mets.
10. Jake Arrieta
11. Kyle Schwarber
12. Daniel Murphy, who said afterwards, "I can't explain what I'm doing." He batted .529 (9-for-17) in the series to be named the NLCS MVP.
13. 42-year-old pitcher Bartolo Colon recorded his first postseason win since 2001. According to STATS it had been 14 years, 12 days between postseason victories for Colon, topping the previous record of exactly 14 years by Milt Wilcox.
14. True
15. 0–7

Fourteen

The Strange and the Bizarre

If you're a die-hard Cubs fan you might want to skip this part. We understand. So many years of heartbreak and so many near-misses and unusual occurrences that not everyone wants to recall them all over and over again. So to try to help we've put most of the strange and unusual aspects of Cubs history in this one section, including the curse.

Baseball fans are a fickle lot to begin with and curses are one way they explain everything from odd bounces to championship droughts. The Curse of the Black Sox and the Curse of the Bambino have come and gone, but Cubs fans are still dealing with having not won a World Series since 1908.

Most call it the Curse of the Billy Goat, which we'll get into in a moment, but some of the things fans have done in an attempt to snap the curse include:

- Numerous goats have been brought to Wrigley Field.
- In 2003, the Year of the Goat in China, a group of Cubs fans took a goat named "Virgil Homer" to Houston to try and redirect the curse to the Astros.

- A butchered goat was hung from the Harry Caray statue at Wrigley Field in 2007.
- A Greek Orthodox priest sprayed holy water in and around the Cubs dugout during the 2008 playoffs.
- In 2012 a group of five Chicago Cubs fans calling themselves "Crack the Curse" walked from the team's spring training home in Mesa, Arizona, to Wrigley Field. They brought along a goat and raised money for the Fred Hutchison Cancer Research Facility.
- In 2015 five Cubs fans consumed a 40-pound goat in 13 minutes and 22 seconds.

 # The Strange and the Bizarre

1. What famous play between the Cubs and Giants occurred on September 23, 1908?
2. How old was the player who it's named after at the time?
3. True or false, he would later play for the Cubs.
4. What was his nickname?
5. True or false, the Cubs went on to win the World Series.
6. True of false, the Cubs haven't won the World Series since then.
7. What's named after the play and located about a block away from Wrigley Field?
8. Who supposedly put the goat curse on the Cubs in 1945?
9. Why?
10. What's the goat's name?
11. How many consecutive times had the Cubs lost in the World Series before losing in 1945?
12. What allegedly cursed the Cubs in 1969?

13. What do Mets fans call that year's team?
14. Who did the Cubs blow a two-game lead to in the five-of-five 1984 National League Championships Series?
15. Who hit a home run in the bottom of the ninth of Game 4 to tie the series?
16. Who had a sharp ground ball go under his glove for an error that helped the Padres win Game 5?
17. What was first baseman Bill Buckner wearing under his fielding glove when he made the famous error with the ball going between his legs during Game 6 of the 1986 World Series?
18. What was the score heading into the eighth inning of Game 6 in the 2003 National League Championship Series against the Florida Marlins?
19. Which player was leaping and trying to make a reaching catch in the stands only to have a fan deflect the ball away?
20. Who misplayed what could have been a double-play ball two batters later?

Answers

1. The play was called Merkle's Boner and the Baseball Almanac gives the following description: "The Cubs and Giants were locked in a furious pennant battle. On September 23, 1908, the score was tied 1–1 with two out in the last of the ninth inning at the Polo Grounds. Runners were on first and third base when Al Bridwell singled to center. As the runner on third crossed the plate with the apparent winning run, Fred Merkle jogged towards second base then started for the clubhouse in right field, leaving the basepaths. The Cubs retrieved the ball (or a ball), tossed it to Johnny Evers who tagged second, and a force out was called ending the game in a tie." The game was replayed on Oct. 8. The Cubs won 4–2 to clinch the pennant to advance to the World Series.
2. 19
3. True. Merkle played another 14 years including with the Cubs from 1917–20.
4. Bonehead
5. True
6. True
7. Merkle's Bar & Grill
8. Billy Goat Tavern owner Billy Sianis.
9. Because he and his goat were kicked out of Game 4 of the World Series due to the smell of the goat. Depending on which version you go by, the order supposedly came down from owner Phillip K. Wrigley and Sianis was heard saying on his way out, "The Cubs ain't gonna win no more. The Cubs will never win a World Series so long as the goat is not allowed in Wrigley Field." The Cubs led the series 2–1, only to lose three of the last four games to the Detroit Tigers. Sianis' family claims he subsequently sent a telegram to Wrigley that said "Who Stinks Now?"
10. Murphy
11. Six: 1910, 1918 1929, 1932, 1935 and 1938. It hasn't returned to the World Series since 1945.
12. A black cat that ran out on to the field in front of the Cubs dugout at Shea Stadium on Sept. 9th. It ran circles around Ron Santo in the on-deck circle and then vanished underneath the stands.
13. The Miracle Mets. The Cubs blew a 9½-game lead in the standings.
14. The San Diego Padres.
15. Steve Garvey
16. First baseman Leon Durham
17. His old Cubs batting glove.
18. The Cubs led 3–0
19. Moises Alou
20. Alex Gonzalez. The Marlins ended up scoring eight runs in the inning and went on to win the series in seven games.

Fifteen

Miscellaneous

From the stadiums to the World Series and the Hall of Famers, just about every aspect of the Chicago Cubs has been covered, right?

Hardly.

This section will test your knowledge of everything else in a very random way, from the odd moments to the unusual statistics that just don't quite fit in anywhere else.

 Miscellaneous

1. What was the longest home winning streak to start a season in Cubs history?
2. What was the longest losing streak to start a season?
3. Who made the most Opening Day starts for the Cubs?
4. True or false, when the Cubs participated in the highest scoring game in Major League history in 1922, they nearly blew a 19-run lead.
5. Which team did the Cubs face in the Major League's highest-scoring game since 1922?
6. In 1956, what did Jim Davis become just the third pitcher in National League history to do?

7. In 1906 how many consecutive 1–0 games did the Cubs play?

8. How long did it take to play the 2–1 loss to the Dodgers at Wrigley Field on August 17–18, 1982?

9. What's the Cubs' record for longest game played in terms of innings?

10. When Sammy Sosa hit 66 home runs in 1998, who did he hit the last one off of (and two earlier in the season)?

11. On Sept. 14, 1908, the Cubs and Reds combined for 29 hits. How many of them were for extra bases?

12. Why did pitcher Claude Passeau play with a special modified glove?

13. Who set the National League record for home runs hit by a catcher with 37 in 1930?

14. Who filed a $450,000 grievance against Major League Baseball and owner William Wrigley following a career-ending arm injury in 1944?

15. Which Cub is one of only two pitchers in Major League history who has won two games that went at least 18 innings during one season?

16. What was Anthony Rizzo diagnosed with in April 2008, before he joined the Cubs?

17. Who did Greg Maddux strike out to notch No. 3,000 of his career on July 26, 2005?

18. Name the four Japanese-born players in Cubs history.

19. What's the single-season record for home runs hit at Wrigley Field (by the Cubs and opponents)?

20. Name the only two Cubs to hit grand slams on their birthdays.

21. Who was the oldest person to ever play for the Cubs?

22. Name the only three players who started on Opening Day when in their 40s?

23. Twice in Cubs history the team won 16 consecutive games behind a pitcher starting at Wrigley Field, who in both cases went 13–0 in those games during the streak. Name them.

24. What's the Wrigley Field record for consecutive victories by a pitcher?

25. How many home runs did the Cubs hit during a three-game series at Colorado on August 10–12, 2002 to tie a National League record?
26. In 1886 how many consecutive decisions did Jim McCormick win at the start of the season?
27. How many scoreless innings did the Cubs and Astros play before one of the teams won 1–0 at Wrigley Field on May 31, 2003?
28. Who are the only two Cubs to win the Roberto Clemente Award?
29. Who was the youngest person to ever play for the Cubs?
30. Who was the first switch-hitter in Cubs history?
31. Who are the only three Cubs to hit three extra-inning home runs in one season?
32. Who was the first Cubs player to hit a home run during his first Major League at-bat?
33. Who is the only Chicago Cub to hit grand slams in consecutive games?
34. Who has hit the most grand slams in Cubs history?
35. What's the only tandem in Cubs history to hit back-to-back home runs twice in the same game?
36. What's the only tandem in Cubs history to throw back-to-back one-hitters?
37. Who combined to record the only multiple grand slam inning in Cubs history?
38. When Jake Arrieta won the Cy Young Award in 2015, what was his ERA during the second half of the season?
39. Who is credited with hitting the first pinch-hit home run in franchise history?
40. Who hit the Cubs' only inside-the-park grand slam since 1951?

Answers

1. 21 games in 1880.
2. 14 games in 1997.
3. Cap Anson with 16, the last of which was in 1895.
4. True. After a 10-run second inning followed by a 14-run fourth, the Cubs led 25–6, and ended up winning 26–23. The Phillies had the bases loaded when the last out was recorded.
5. The Phillies, again on May 17, 1979. The Cubs had trailed 21–9, but rallied and tied the score in the eighth inning before Mike Schmidt hit a game-winning home run in the 10th for an unorthodox 23–22 victory.
6. Strike out four batters in one inning.
7. Four, which were part of a team record nine-game stretch of games decided by one run from June 24–July 4.
8. Six hours and 10 minutes.
9. 22, a 4–3 victory over Boston at Braves Field on May 17, 1927.
10. Jose Lima
11. None.
12. He had a deformed left hand that was disfigured by a childhood shooting accident.
13. Gabby Hartnett
14. Boyd Tepler
15. Ed Reulbach (according to the Elias Sports Bureau). Mets pitcher Tom Gorman was the other in 1985.
16. Hodgkin's lymphoma.
17. San Francisco's Omar Vizquel.
18. Outfielders Kosuke Fukudome and So Taguchi, right-handed pitcher Kyuji Fujikawa and left-handed pitcher Hisanori Takahashi.
19. 233 in 2004 (137 by the Cubs, which was the most they've ever hit at home during a season there as well)
20. Derrek Lee on September 6, 2006 against the Pirates, and Aramis Ramirez on June 25, 2005 at the White Sox.
21. Hoyt Wilhelm. He joined the team in September 1970, two months after his 47th birthday, and pitched in three games.
22. Cap Anson, Dutch Leonard and Gary Gaetti.
23. Lon Warneke (May 27, 1932–April 18, 1933), and Jon Lieber (May 24, 2011–May 6, 2002).
24. 15, set by Bill Lee from September 7, 1935–August 26, 1936, when he made 17 starts.
25. 15
26. 16
27. The Cubs finally scored in the 16th inning (so the answer is 15).
28. Rick Sutcliffe in 1987 and Sammy Sosa in 1998.
29. Milt Scott, who was 16 years and eight months old when he made his Major League debut on September 30, 1882.
30. Player/manager Bob Ferguson in 1878.
31. Ernie Banks (1955), Ron Santo (1966) and Alex Gonzalez (2003).
32. Paul Gillespie, September 11, 1942 at the New York Giants.

33. Sammy Sosa, July 27–28, 1998 at Arizona (and the author can verify this answer as he was there for both of them).
34. Ernie Banks with 12.
35. Ernie Banks and Dee Fondy, who did it in the second and sixth innings at St. Louis on April 16, 1955.
36. Jon Lieber (May 24, 2001 vs. Cincinnati) and Kerry Wood (May 25, 2001, vs. Milwaukee).
37. Tom Burns and Malachi Kittridge both hit grand slams off of Pittsburgh's Bill Phillips in the fifth inning on April 18, 1915.
38. 0.75, the lowest in Major League history.
39. Wilbur Good on June 19, 1913, off Philadelphia's Grover Alexander at Chicago's West Side Grounds.
40. Chico Walker on August 28, 1991 at San Francisco.

Sixteen

The Hot Box

We'll sort of ease you into this.

When Phil Cavarretta was named the National League's most valuable player in 1945 he batted .355 and tallied 97 RBIs despite having only six home runs. He beat out a player from another team who led the league in hits, doubles, home runs, total bases and slugging percentage.

So who was that person and name the seven teammates of Cavarretta, in order, who received MVP votes that year.

If you can get that correct there may be something wrong with you.

Answer: Boston's Tommy Holmes finished second while the teammates were Andy Pafko (fourth), Hank Borowy (sixth), Hank Wyse (seventh), Stan Hack (11th), Claude Passeau (19th), Don Johnson (21st), and Peanuts Lowrey (26th). A total of 33 different players received votes.

When it comes to Chicago Cubs trivia, these are some of the hardest of the hard, the ones that even the staunchest fans will struggle with and say: "Are you kidding me?"

The Hot Box

1. As previously noted Ernie Banks was the first player in baseball history to hit five grand slams in a single season, 1955. Who were the pitchers he hit them against?

2. Among former National League teams the Cubs franchise had a losing record against just two. Name them.

3. Name the first Cubs to be born in the following foreign countries: Bahamas, Cuba, Dominican Republic, Germany, Ireland, Italy, Jamaica, Mexico, Nicaragua, Panama, Poland, Scotland, Singapore, South Korea, Venezuela.

4. Name the first 10 Cubs to hit for the cycle in a game.

5. When Kerry Wood struck out 20 batters on May 6, 1998, who were the only two Houston Astros to reach base?

6. Name the four pitchers who previously held the National League record with 19 strikeouts, the two who held the rookie record with 18, and the only other pitcher who notched as many strikeouts in a game as his age.

7. With his book by the same title, Mudcat Grant invented the term "Black Aces" for African-American pitchers who have won at least 20 games in a season. In addition to Hall of Famers Ferguson Jenkins and Bob Gibson, name the other nine members of this organized group.

8. Which two players went 13 years between stints with the Cubs?

9. What's the longest span a Cub went between home runs?

10. Name all of the Cubs to win the National League's Rookie of the Year award.

11. Name all of the Cubs to be named the National League's MVP.

12. Name all of the Cubs' spring training sites since 1900.

13. Name the eight Cubs who have won at least one Silver Slugger award and the position that's still looking for the first.

14. Billy Williams is one of only seven players in baseball history to have played 1,000 consecutive games, reaching 1,117. Name the other six.

15. On April 9, 2003, the Cubs were involved in a game that featured 27 strikeouts, the most in any Major League nine-inning game that didn't include a walk. Name the three pitchers who contributed at Wrigley Field.

16. The 1986 Mets are one of only 11 teams since 1900 to win 108 games during a single season. Name the other 10.

17. On July 17, 1918, the Cubs participated in game that set a Major League record for longest game without a single error, 21 innings. Name the opponent.

18. When Rick Renteria was selected in the first round of the 1980 June draft by the Pittsburgh Pirates at No. 20 overall, he began a stretch in which four of five draft selections went on to become Major League managers or general managers. Name the other three and the teams that made the selections.

19. Matt Alexander was one of 54 Major League players who served in the military during the Vietnam War. Name them.

20. Name the top four home run hitters among Cubs pitchers.

21. Who are the eight Cubs pitchers who threw a shutout while making their Major League debuts?

22. Who was the first Cub to hit an inside-the-park home run at Wrigley Field as his first Major League home run?

23. Who were the players who hit the only back-to-back inside-the-park home runs in franchise history?

24. Only once since the advent of divisional play in 1969 have the Cubs had the starting pitcher strike out 10 batters in three straight games. Name them.

25. Who turned the only unassisted triple play in Cubs history?

26. When Billy Williams recorded the only natural cycle (single, double, triple, home run in order) in franchise history on July 17, 1966, who were the pitchers?

27. Name the eight father-son combinations to play for the Cubs.

28. In 2013, Jerry Hairston Jr. (2005–06) and Scott Hairston (2013) became the 11th combination of brothers to play for the Cubs. Name the first 10.

29. From 1876 to 2013 there were 79 Cubs who were either born, or went to high school, in the Chicago area. Of them name the 13 who played more than two seasons with the club since 1900.

30. Led by Ernie Banks there are 14 Major League players since 1903 who played in at least 2,000 regular-season games but never participated in a postseason game. Name the other 13.

Answers

1. May 11 off Russ Meyer, May 29 off Lew Burdette, July 17 off Ron Negray, August 2 off Dick Littlefield, and September 19 off Lindy McDaniel.

2. Chicago was 38–60 against the original Baltimore Orioles (1892-99), and 10–12 against the Hartford Dark Blues (1876–1880).

3. Bahamas: Andre Rodgers, 1961–64
   Cuba: Mike Gonzalez, 1925–29
   Dominican Republic: Roberto Pena, 1965–66
   Germany: Ed Eiteljorge, 1890
   Ireland: Jimmy Hallinan, 1877–78
   Italy: Julio Bonetti, 1940
   Jamaica: Rolando Roomes, 1988
   Mexico: Jesse Flores, 1942
   Nicaragua: Porfirio Altamirano, 1984
   Panama: Adolfo Phillips, 1966–69
   Poland: Moe Drabowsky, 1956–60
   Scotland: Hugh Nicol, 1881–82
   Singapore: Robin Jennings, 1996–97
   South Korea: Hee Seop Choi, 2002–03
   Venezuela: Roberto Rodriguez, 1970

4. Jimmy Ryan (twice), Hack Wilson, Babe Herman, Roy Smalley, Lee Walls, Billy Williams, Randy Hundley, Ivan DeJesus, Andre Dawson and Mark Grace

5. Ricky Gutierrez singled and Craig Biggio was hit by a pitch.

6. Providence's Charlie Sweeney (June 7, 1884), St. Louis' Steve Carlton (September 15, 1969), New York's Tom Seaver (April 22, 1970), and New York's David Cone (October 6, 1991); the rookies were Philadelphia's Jack Coombs (September 1, 1906) and Montreal's Bill Gullickson (September 10, 1980); and Bob Feller struck out his age with 17 on September 13, 1936. Gullickson's game was against the Cubs.

7. Vida Blue, Al Downing, Dwight Gooden, Sam Jones, Don Newcombe, Mike Norris, J.R. Richard,

Dave Stewart and Earl Wilson.

8. Roger Bresnahan (1900, 1913–15) and Johnny Moore (1928–29, 1931–32, 1945).

9. Billy Jurges at nine years, 22 days, from August 2, 1938 to August 24, 1947. Jurges was a Cub from 1931–38 and 1946–47, and both home runs were hit at the Polo Grounds.

10. Billy Williams in 1961, Ken Hubbs in 1962, Jerome Walton in 1989, Kerry Wood in 1998, Geovany Soto in 2008, Kris Bryant in 2015.

11. Frank Schulte in 1911, Rogers Hornsby in 1929, Gabby Hartnett in 1935, Phil Cavarretta in 1945, Hank Sauer in 1952, Ernie Banks in 1958 and 1959; Ryne Sandberg in 1984, Andre Dawson in 1987, Sammy Sosa in 1998

12. Selma, Alabama (1900)
    Champaign, Illinois (1901–02)
    Los Angeles, California (1903–04)
    Santa Monica, California (1905)
    West Baden, Indiana (1906–08)
    Shreveport, Louisiana (1909)
    West Baden, Indiana (1910–11)
    New Orleans, Louisiana (1912)
    Tampa, Florida (1913–16)
    Pasadena, California (1917–20)
    Catalina Island, California (1921–41; 1946–51)
    French Lick, Indiana (1942–45)
    Mesa, Arizona (1952–65, 1979–present)
    Long Beach, California (1966)
    Scottsdale, Arizona (1967–78)

13. Leon Durham, Ryne Sandberg, Andre Dawson, Sammy Sosa, Michael Barrett, Derrek Lee, Carlos Zambrano and Aramis Ramirez. No Cubs shortstops have won the award.

14. Cal Ripken, Jr. (2,632 games), Lou Gehrig (2,130), Everett Scott (1,307), Steve Garvey (1,207), Miguel Tejada (1,152), and Joe Sewell (1,103 GP).

15. Mark Prior struck out 12 Montreal Expos, while Javier Vazquez (14) and Luis Ayala (one) struck out 15 Cubs.

16. 1906 Cubs, 2001 Mariners, 1998 Yankees, 1954 Indians, 1909 Pirates, 1927 Yankees, 1961 Yankees, 1969 Orioles, 1970 Orioles and 1975 Reds.

17. The Philadelphia Phillies

18. No. 22 Terry Francona by the Montreal Expos, Billy Beane by the New York Mets, and John Gibbons, also by the Mets. Francona played for the Cubs in 1986.

19. Vic Albury, Matt Alexander, Frank Baker, Jim Bibby, Larry Biittner, Gene Brabender, Al Bumbry, Darrel Chaney, Bruce Christensen, Mike Davison, Ed Figueroa, Rich Folkers, Ted Ford, Larry French, Wayne Garrett, Roy Gleason, Chuck Goggin, Dave Goltz, Doug Griffin, Tom Heintzelman, Phil Hennigan, Jim Holt, Mike Jackson, Ray Jarvis, Bob Johnson, Bob Jones, Jerry Kenney, Jim Kern, Jerry Koosman, John Lowenstein, Garry Maddox, Jim Magnuson, Gene Martin, Larry Miller, George Mitterwald, Curt Motton, Thurman Munson, Bobby Murcer, Ray Newman, Scott Northey, Darrell Osteen, Harry Parker, Hal Quick, Dave Schneck, Mickey Scott, Rich Severson, Fred Stanley, Leroy Stanton, Earl Stephenson, Jim Strickland, Champ Summers, Jerry Terrell,

Floyd Wicker, George Zeber. Source: Baseball Almanac.

20. Carlos Zambrano (23), Fergie Jenkins (13), Claude Passeau (12) and Charlie Root (11).

21. Albert Spalding, April 25, 1876 at Louisville; John Hibbard, July 31, 1884 vs. Detroit; George Borchers, May 18, 1888 vs. Boston Braves; Frank Dwyer, September 20, 1888 vs. Washington; Bill Phyle, September 17, 1898 at Washington; Alex Hardy, September 4, 1902 at Brooklyn; Leonard Cole, October 6, 1909 at St. Louis; Jeff Pico, May 31, 1988 vs. Cincinnati.

22. Tony Campana on August 5, 2011.

23. Eddie Waitkus and Marv Rickert against the New York Giants at the Polo Grounds on June 23, 1946.

24. Ken Holtzman (vs. San Francisco), Fergie Jenkins (vs. San Diego) and Dick Selma (vs. San Diego) from May 11–13, 1969.

25. Shortstop Jimmy Cooney at Pittsburgh on May 30, 1927.

26. The single was off Art Mahaffey, the double and triple were against Don Dennis, and the home run came off Hal Woodeshick.

27. Bobby Adams (1957–59) and Mike Adams (1976–77);
Joe Coleman (1976) and Casey Coleman (2010–12);
Jimmy Cooney (1890–92) and Jimmy Cooney (1926–27);
Herm Doscher (1879) and Jack Doscher (1903);
Randy Hundley (1966–73, 1976–77) and Todd Hundley (2001–02);
Marty Keough (1966) and Matt Keough (1986);
Gary Matthews (1984–87) and Gary Matthews, Jr. (2000–01);
Chris Speier (1985–86) and Justin Speier (1998)

28. Danny Breeden (1971) and Hal Breeden (1971);
Kid Camp (1894) and Lew Camp (1893–94);
Mort Cooper (1949) and Walker Cooper (1954–55);
Larry Corcoran (1880–85) and Mike Corcoran (1884);
Sammy Drake (1960–61) and Solly Drake (1956);
Jiggs Parrott (1892–95) and Tom Parrott (1893);
Eric Patterson (2007) and Corey Patterson (2000–05);
Rick Reuschel (1972–81, 1983–84) and Paul Reuschel (1975–78);
Ed Sauer (1943–45) and Hank Sauer (1949–55);
Jim Tyrone (1972, 1974–75) and Wayne Tyrone (1976)

29. Cliff Aberson (1947–49); Phil Cavarretta (1934–53); Neal Cotts (2007–09); Jim Fanning (1954–57); Chick Fraser (1907–09); Roy Henshaw (1933, 35–36); Don Johnson (1943–48); Tony Kaufmann (1921–27); Emil Kush (1941–42, 46–49); Bill McCabe (1918–20); John Ostrowski (1943–46); Chico Walker (1985–87, 91–92); Randy Wells (2008–12).

30. After Banks with 2,528 games, they are, in order: Luke Appling (2,422), Mickey Vernon (2,409), Buddy Bell (2,405), Ron Santo (2,243), Joe Torre (2,209), Toby Harrah (2,155), Harry Heilmann (2,147), Eddie Yost (2,109), Roy McMillan (2,093), Don Kessinger (2,078), George Sisler (2,055), Cy Williams (2,002), and Adam Dunn (2,001).

About the Author

Christopher Walsh has been an award-winning sportswriter since 1990 and has authored 24 books. He's been twice nominated for a Pulitzer Prize, won three Football Writers Association of America awards, and received both the 2006 and 2014 Herby Kirby Memorial Award, the Alabama Sports Writers Association's highest honor for story of the year. Originally from Minnesota and a graduate of the University of New Hampshire, he currently works for Bleacher Report and resides in Tuscaloosa, Alabama.

His other books include:

Sweet 16: Alabama's Historic 2015 Championship Season, 2016

Mets Triviology, 2016

Red Sox Triviology, 2016

Nick Saban vs. College Football, 2014.

100 Things Crimson Tide Fans Need to Know & Do Before They Die, 2008; updated 2012

Cowboys Triviology, 2011

Packers Triviology, 2011

Steelers Triviology, 2011

Huddle Up: New York Giants Football, 2009.

Huddle Up: Alabama Football, 2009.

Huddle Up: Michigan Football, 2009.

Huddle Up: Notre Dame Football, 2009.

Huddle Up: Ohio State Football, 2009.

Huddle Up: Oklahoma Football, 2009.

Huddle Up: Tennessee Football, 2009.

Huddle Up: Texas Football, 2009.

Who's No. 1? 100-Plus Years of Controversial Champions in College Football, 2007.

Where Football is King: A History of the SEC, 2006.

No Time Outs: What It's Really Like to be a Sportswriter Today, 2006.

Crimson Storm Surge: Alabama Football, Then and Now, 2005.

Return to Glory: The Story of Alabama's 2008 Season, 2009 (contributing writer).